KANGAROOS
The Marvelous Mob

KANGAROOS
The Marvelous Mob

TEXT BY
Terry Domico

PHOTOGRAPHS BY
Terry Domico and Mark Newman

☑ Facts On File

KANGAROOS: The Marvelous Mob
Copyright © 1993 by Terry Domico
Photographs copyright by Terry Domico and Mark Newman

Facts On File, Inc.
460 Park Avenue South
New York NY 10016

Library of Congress Cataloging-in-Publication Data

Domico, Terry
Kangaroos : the marvelous mob / text by Terry Domico ; photographs by Terry Domico
and Mark Newman.
p. cm.
Includes bibliographical references and index.
ISBN 0-8160-2360-3
1. Kangaroos. I. Title.
QL737.M35D66 1993
599.2—dc20 92-38772

A British CIP catalogue record for this book is available from the British Library.

Facts On File books are available at special discounts when purchased in bulk quantities for
businesses, associations, institutions or sales promotions. Please contact our Special Sales
Department in New York at 212/683-2244 or 800/322-8755.

Text design by Ron Monteleone
Cartography by Marc Greene
Composition by Facts On File, Inc.
Manufactured by Mandarin Offset
Printed in Hong Kong

10 9 8 7 6 5 4 3 2 1

This book is printed on acid-free paper.

For the Australian people . . .

CONTENTS

PREFACE

In the inventory of this planet's exotic creatures, few seem as extraordinary as the kangaroo. If you had never seen or heard of one before, it is very likely you wouldn't believe me if I were to describe this animal with such outrageous proportions: a man-sized animal with a deer-like head, rabbit-like ears, grasshopper-like hind legs and tiny squirrel-like forelegs that is able to jump over 35 feet (11 meters) in a single bound and deliver karate chops to its rivals. Sound amazing? Kangaroos and their successful survival in this modern world are, indeed.

Australia is famous as the home of the kangaroo. About the size of the continental United States, it is also one of the globe's oldest landmasses. That ancient monolith called Ayer's Rock is evidence of some 600 million years of nature's sculpture. Kangaroos have been here (and in New Guinea and Tasmania) for at least 15 million of those years.

Australia is also a very young land in terms of its human development. While the native Aborigines lived and hunted for thousands of years in one of the world's oldest cultures, European settlement only began in the late 18th century. But within this short span of time, white man's "progress" has permanently altered the design of existence for all other life in this Land Down Under.

When cophotographer Mark Newman and I stumbled, jet-lagged, off the plane in Sydney to begin our work of assessing and chronicling kangaroos, we had no idea of the adventures ahead that would forever transform our own view of this island continent.

The first one began almost immediately. We needed transportation to explore wild Australia and its outback roads, so we bought a car. It was a lemon-colored station wagon that seemed to run pretty well and, best of all, it was cheap.

Having gotten wheels under us, the next question was where do we go? The answer was deceptively easy. Everyone we asked pointed in the same general

Opposite: Red-necked wallaby

direction, "Out there." Now, after more than a year of exploration, I've come to appreciate Australia's vast expanses. "Outback" distances can humorously reflect the isolation of its far-flung communities.

"The research station?" the petrol-station attendant mused. "Well, it's up that way," pointing, "just around the corner, mate. You can't miss it."

You might have guessed what happened. "Just around the corner" turned out to be an all-day, 135-mile (215-kilometer) drive over some of the roughest terrain ever to be laughingly called a road.

We did find kangaroos, however . . . plenty of them. Australia is lucky to be one of the few places left on the planet where wildlife still outnumber people and their domestic animals.

My first kangaroo, or 'roo, sighting is an indelible memory. We were driving along a dirt road through flat sheep-ranching country in central New South Wales. The monotonous landscape was relieved only by isolated clumps of eucalyptus trees and occasional fences angling off on endless tangents. Finding a nice spot to make an evening camp was the only thought occupying our weary minds.

Suddenly a troop of six Grey kangaroos bounced across the road in front of the vehicle and alongside the driver's door, pacing the car. For a few moments we stared, wide-eyed, at their loping bodies. The setting sun outlined their furry coats with a halo of golden light. Over the road noise I could hear the soft "thump . . . thump . . ." as their feet hit the ground and we could almost reach out and touch the nearest animal. Abruptly the group changed direction and easily jumped the fence bordering the road. Slamming on the brakes, we slid to a dusty standstill just in time to watch them stop a hundred yards away, look back at us and then, one by one, disappear into the darkening woods.

Fleeting visions of wild kangaroos have enchanted dozens of generations of people who have been lucky enough to experience them. Unfortunately, kangaroos are also phantoms of exasperation to the many farmers and stock graziers who try to tame this land in their struggle to make a living. They perceive them as pests and a direct threat to their efforts. Literally millions of the animals are killed each year as a result. This polarity of views has fueled a long-festering emotional controversy within Australian society and in other countries where wildlife conservation is of great concern. Almost no one, we soon learned, is neutral about kangaroos.

As far as understanding the wildlife we share this planet with, we're living in an era of heightened awareness. Biologists have learned more about kangaroos and other wildlife in the last 30 years than throughout all the rest of human history. It's also ironic, during this time of enlightenment, that so many of the world's species are vanishing. *KANGAROOS: The Marvelous Mob*, then, is an account of their survival in this changing time. It is also the captivating story of the animals themselves.

All scientific names and terms included in this book are those currently in use. Although most of the information presented is generally accepted as fact, some biological concepts and behaviors are not well understood. In these cases, I will try to present one or two interpretations by other experts in addition to my own. I hope that this book will act as a kind of catalyst for new thought as well as a good reference for what we already know.

Terry Domico,
San Juan Islands, Washington

ACKNOWLEDGMENTS

Few books are the result of a single person's efforts. There were numerous people who contributed, sometimes unknowingly, in the preparation of this book. I would like to give special tribute to a few without whose help this volume may never have come into existence. Thanks to Dr. Michael Archer for trading books and steering me in the right directions; to Ray and Anne Williams for your generous hospitality and for allowing me to stay at "Motel" Cowan; to Martin O'Malley for your hospitality and for introducing me to the rest of the National Parks and Wildlife Service "gang" in Charleville; to Jim McDonnell, Area Manager for Queensland National Parks and Wildlife Service for allowing me to be part of that gang; to Dr. Tim Clancy for our discussions on "sociality" and the time we got stuck in the sand; to Graeme Moss and Debby Ashworth for exciting evenings of kangaroo stunning and cannon-netting; to Margaret Kubbere of the Featherdale Wildlife Park for allowing us the freedom to roam over your place with our cameras; to Mike Young and Bill Poole of the CSIRO for candid and informative chats on Christmas Eve; to Dr. Gerry Maynes, Director of the National Kangaroo Monitoring Unit, for reviewing the manuscript for "factual" accuracy; to Jeoff Ross for heaps of good contacts and conversations; to Marjorie Wilson of the Kangaroo Protection Co-Op for your efforts at keeping kangaroos a political issue; to Mary Lou Shubert, ABC reporter, for opening your video files to me; to Jeff Vaughan for your good cheer even when you cut off a finger chopping food for the critters; to John Barker for your unflagging enthusiasm; to Ed Stokes for your perspective on early Australian explorers and your exasperation at my getting lost right in your neighborhood; to John Seebeck for your time spent teaching me about potoroos; to Ray and Karen Abernathy for your continuing friendship, which allowed me to feel at home in your home; to Dr. Gordon Grigg for taking time out of your busy schedule to share your ideas with me; to Bill and Pat Bonthrone for your hospitality to a stranger on a quest; to Bob Miles for loaning me the key to the D.P.I. research property and for your generosity when I questioned your study's results; to Ted Heineman and Chris Bryant for introducing me to the world of the professional 'roo shooter; to Lee Werle and Judy Steenburg of the Woodland Park Zoo in Seattle, Washington, for your kindness and help in bringing me up to speed during my first attempts at understanding macropods; to Dr. Tim Flannery for your help in reviewing the macropods of New Guinea; to Geoff Williams and Noel McCracken of the Healesville Sanctuary for allowing free access to your facilities; to Stephen Wild, ethnomusicologist with the Australian Institute of Aboriginal Studies for helping me to locate a special piece of Aboriginal artwork; to Tom Thompson for frank discussions about the kangaroo industry; to Greg Hocking, biologist with the Tasmanian Department of Lands, Parks and Whatever for your help and sympathy for our project; to Ola Hanson, wherever you may be, we will always remember the yellow 1975 Volkswagon station wagon that you sold us and the spare tire that we didn't receive and really needed; to John and Caroline Hamilton, owners of the Tasmanian Devil Park in Taranna, for your hospitality and help in photographing a devil "feeding frenzy"; to Linda Gibson, collection manager for the Australia Museum, for allowing me free access to the museum's macropod skull collection; to John Fletcher, Aboriginal Liaison Officer with the Northern Territories Conservation Commission for introducing me to the Aboriginal way of life and to ranger Barry Scott for taking me there; to Nigel Hunter, Peter Jadbula and Larry Atkinson for sharing your camp and your food; to Caroline Barnes, who quickly taught me that I really didn't need an assistant; to Peter Johnson for helping me with the pronunciation and photography of Hypsiprymnodon; to Dr. Roger Martin for sharing your research camp and your good home brew; to Mark Newman, my cophotographer and coadventurer, for dedicating your time and talent to this project; to Ken Talley for your valuable comments about the text; to my editor, Susan Schwartz, for allowing me room to breathe; and finally, to Andrine, my Malaysian sweetheart, whose letters somehow always found me and brightened many a lonesome day in the outback. She has since become my bride.

I am thankful to have all these people in my life.

A NOTE FROM MARK NEWMAN

L ike many adventurers, I am guilty of spending prodigious amounts of time away from home and family, and for years have been treading the fine line between nature photography and divorce. My marriage has survived expeditions to Borneo, China and Africa. If those places qualified for "away times," what wife's heart, I thought, wouldn't also allow for kangaroos?

So off Terry and I soared on the mother of all flights, California to Australia, 14 hours nonstop. We staggered, jet-lagged and by ignorance, into the Sydney red-light district and got a hotel room. Then we bought a rapidly decomposing car and tried to learn how to drive on the left-hand side of the road. Our adventure Down Under had begun.

This adventure was to include an outback inhabited by 30 species of poisonous snakes, an ascent of Ayers Rock (Uluru), a descent down Katherine Gorge, charging emus, lethal encephalitis ticks (I plucked the last one from my neck while on the plane back to Los Angeles), torrential downpours, world-class drought, otherworldly digiridoo music, Aboriginal corroborrees, wrestling down big Red kangaroos to help attach identifying ear tags, kangaroos around campfires, kangaroos in my tent, bats with three-foot wing spans, birds that scream like ghouls, first-hand reports of Tasmanian tiger sightings, a million rabbits with pinkeye, constant buzzing flies in the face, maggots hatching in our ham sandwiches, "upside-down" constellations, billabong swimming sessions with crocodiles, getting lost in outback 100-degree heat without a compass, temporary blindness, seasickness while heading for an island off Tasmania, and some of the finest beaches, beer and people in the world.

And afterwards? My wife still let me come home.

Mark Newman
Anchorage, Alaska

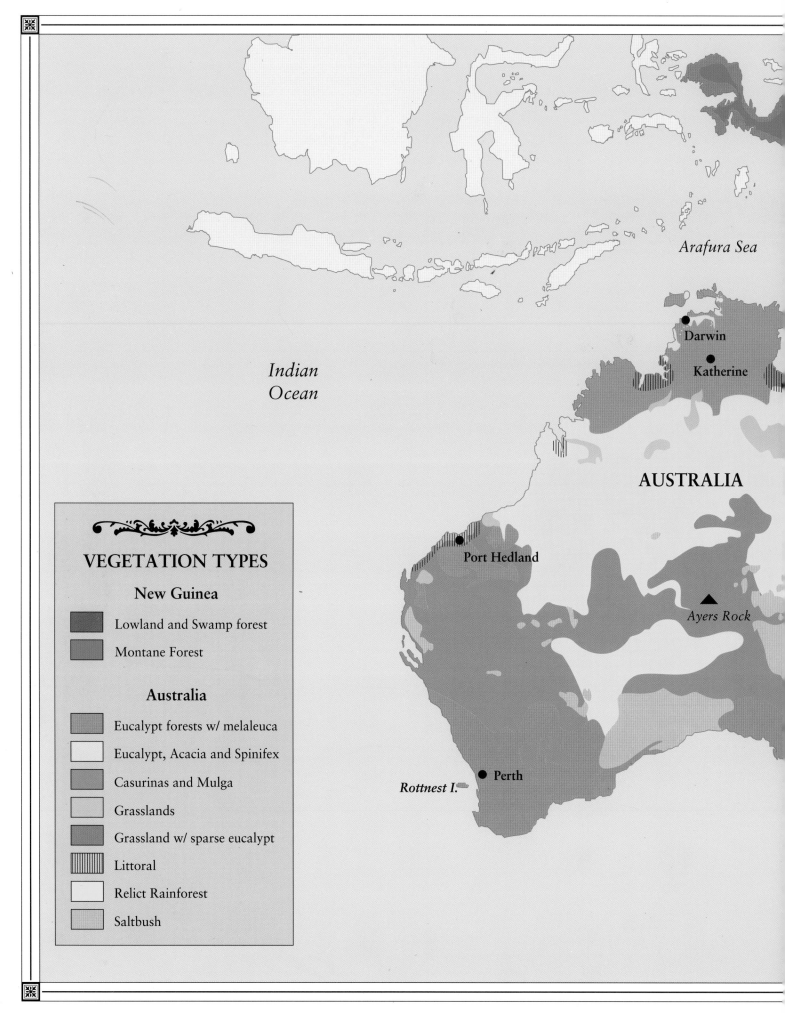

Arafura Sea

Indian Ocean

Darwin

Katherine

AUSTRALIA

Port Hedland

▲
Ayers Rock

● Perth

Rottnest I.

VEGETATION TYPES

New Guinea

Lowland and Swamp forest

Montane Forest

Australia

Eucalypt forests w/ melaleuca

Eucalypt, Acacia and Spinifex

Casurinas and Mulga

Grasslands

Grassland w/ sparse eucalypt

Littoral

Relict Rainforest

Saltbush

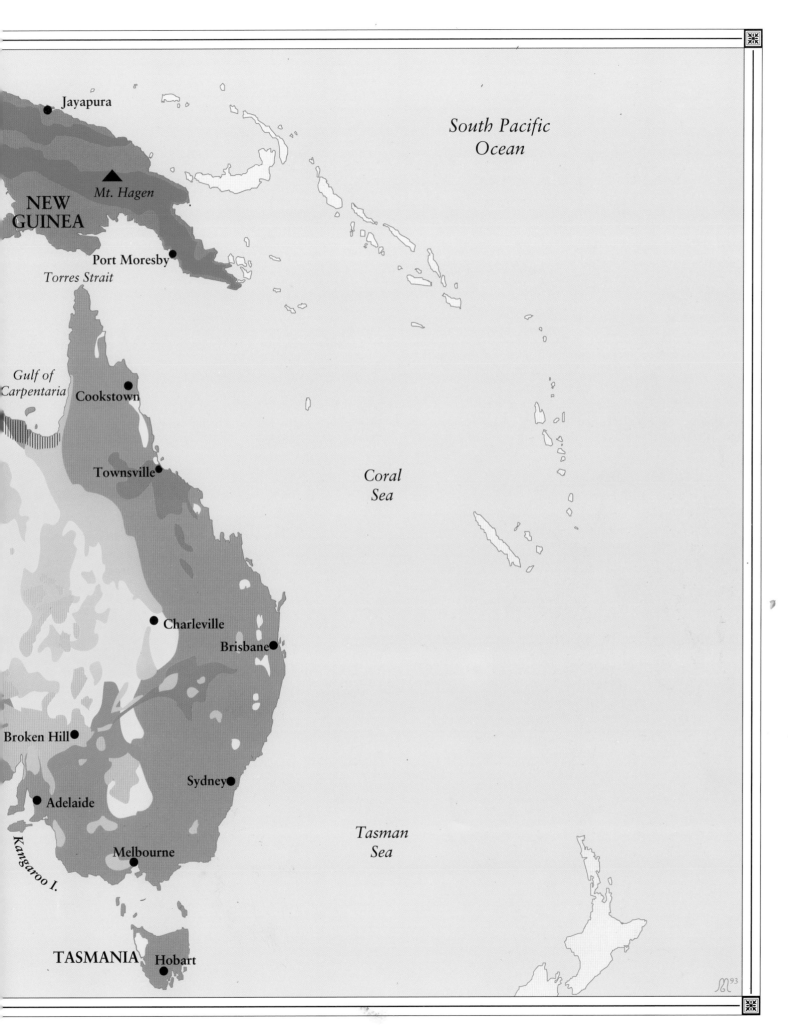

Jayapura

Mt. Hagen ▲

**NEW
GUINEA**

Port Moresby

Torres Strait

*Gulf of
Carpentaria*

Cookstown

Townsville

Broken Hill

Charleville

Brisbane

Sydney

Adelaide

Kangaroo I.

Melbourne

TASMANIA Hobart

*South Pacific
Ocean*

*Coral
Sea*

*Tasman
Sea*

KANGAROOS
The Marvelous Mob

An Amazing Marsupial:

What Is a Kangaroo?

I come from the northern plains
Where the girls and grass are scanty;
Where the creeks run dry or ten feet high
And it's either drought or plenty.

From "The Overlander" (Anon)

Peering through a window of the jetliner for my first glimpse of Australia, I could just discern the thin white line of breakers 40,000 feet (12,200 meters) below where land confronted the sea. I imagined our flickering shadow undulating over millions of rocks, bushes and trees (and perhaps a few kangaroos). Stretching ahead, as far as I could see, was the brownish green of a continent seen from high in the air.

This continent, though, is very different from any other. As a place, it's difficult to classify. Consisting of more than 3 million square miles (7,800,000 square kilometers) of land, it is nearly 2,500 miles (4,000 kilometers) across and stretches north and south from the tropics to the very edge of the Antarctic seas.

Roughly the size of the continental United States, Australia contains a human population that's less than the state of New York. It's considered to be the world's flattest continent, yet it holds significant and spectacular gorges and mountain ranges. It is famous for being an incredibly arid place where rivers run only with sand, but it also has produced some of the world's most outstanding rainforest. And to top it off, summer comes at a time when most other English-speaking nations are experiencing winter.

The first European explorers had a great deal of trouble with "Terra Australis," the Great South Land. They found a world where almost nothing seemed to match their previous experiences or their expectations. Most of the mammals here raised their young in pouches and, stranger still, others laid eggs. To these people, coming from green and temperate climates, Australia's endless parched expanses must have seemed totally alien and hostile.

As late as 1879, that view was still being echoed. An article in the *Illustrated Sydney News* stated, "The whole continent of Australia was found not to possess a single animal worthy of perpetuation."

Opposite: Kangaroo tracks in sand.

This apparent worthlessness inspired the formation of several "acclimatisation" societies within the growing nation. The aim of these societies was to introduce useful and "more appreciated" species of plants and animals into Australia.

In 1864, for example, the New South Wales Society stated its aims as, ". . . stocking our waste waters, woods and plains with choice animals, making that which was dull and lifeless become animated by creatures in full enjoyment of existence and lands before useless become fertile with rare and valuable trees and plants."

There were very few successes with these experiments and (unfortunately) some of the introductions that seemed to work at the time have since become pests of epic proportions. Rabbits, for example, have overrun the entire continent and seriously degraded vast areas of semi-arid land. It's not surprising that these societies quietly faded away.

In Tasmania, this Red-necked wallaby is locally known as the Bennett's wallaby.

Discovery of the Kangaroo

Although the Australian coast had been sighted by Europeans as early as 1605, it wasn't until 1629 that the first kangaroo observation was recorded by a Dutch navigator, Francisco Pelsaert, whose ill-fated ship, *Batavia*, wrecked near the Houtman Abrolhos, a group of islands off Western Australia.

While stranded, Pelsaert also made some of the first notes about kangaroo reproduction. He wrote that its pouch young "were only the size of a bean, though at the same time perfectly proportioned." He never did know what to call them; the name "kangaroo" hadn't been coined yet.

In the decades following Pelsaert's misadventure (he lived to tell his tale of mutiny and hardship) more and more European ships came to visit Australian shores. It wasn't until after 1770, however, that the word "kangaroo" began to be generally known, when, as legend has it, Captain Cook and his party asked an Aborigine what the creature was called.

There is now evidence that suggests that the term "kangaroo" actually meant "I don't understand" in that particular native's language. Whatever its original intention, however, "kangaroo" soon became the first and probably most wide-spread Aboriginal term ever incorporated into the English tongue. The discovery of kangaroos caused a great sensation in Europe. Their outrageous proportions were so curious that everyone, even the skeptics, wanted to see one. After several failed attempts, a live one arrived in Britain from the Land Down Under in 1791. Londoners practically stormed the Lyceum Theatre to see it.

The Naturalists Arrive

The next 100 years were exciting (and tough) times for Australian exploration and expansion. Numerous expeditions proposing to explore its interior ended in failure. But the few that did succeed occasionally brought back preserved collections of amazing plant and animal material. There were problems communicating these finds to the rest of the world, though.

"If you look at early drawings of Australian fauna," says Bill Poole, a contemporary Australian biologist, "many of the larger animals were drawn from flat skins from museum specimens. The proportions are *really* a bit peculiar. Also, most of the drawings' backgrounds tend to have a European flavor, rather than Australian, because they were painted in England."

There were exceptions, of course. One was John Gould, an English naturalist, whose large, lavishly illustrated books on birds commanded ever-increasing prices among bibliophiles. These volumes were so successful that in 1838 he and his wife moved to Australia for a couple of years.

He quickly set up shop, hiring various hunters and trappers to help amass a large collection of birds and mammals. Being a good entrepreneur, Gould lined up the landed gentry (who could afford these sorts of things) to subscribe to his forthcoming books, *The Birds of Australia* (1840–48) in seven volumes and *Mammals of Australia* (1845–63) in three volumes. These systematic works for which he is best known were produced in serial installments to an eagerly awaiting audience.

John Gould's luscious paintings finally gave the world its first detailed and intimate look at the wonders of Australian wildlife. Now a national treasure, these plates are still occasionally reproduced in modern books and magazines. With gloved hands, I once had the honor of turning through one of his original volumes.

Although the "civilized" world now knew what kangaroos looked like, there was still very little detailed information available about them. Mr. T. Penant's 1871

History of Quadrupeds summed up the world's knowledge in one concentrated paragraph:

> It inhabits the western side of New Holland [one of many early names for Australia], and has yet been discovered in no other part of the world. It lurks among grass; feeds on vegetables; goes entirely on its hind legs, making use of the forefeet only for digging, or bringing its food to its mouth. The dung is like that of a deer. It is timid: at the sight of a man flies from them by amazing leaps, springing over bushes seven or eight feet high; and going progressively from rock to rock. It carries its tail at right angles with its body when in motion; and when it alights often looks back; it is much too swift for greyhounds; it is very good eating.

The last sentence was especially important. In the early days of Australian settlement, kangaroos were viewed first as food, then as curiosities. It was not long, however, before they came to be regarded as running quarry for sportsmen and later as pests to be exterminated.

A BIG STEP BACK IN TIME

Today's kangaroos still represent all of these things to the people they live near. But just how did the animals come to be in the first place? It's a very old story, so old in fact, that it's become part of Australia's bedrock. Unfortunately the threads of testimony are sketchy here and there, so much of the plot is still theory. It begins somewhere in the dim past, perhaps more than 250 million years ago.

At that time all of the earth's continents may have been united into a single land mass called Pangaea. We don't know this for sure, but there is considerable supporting evidence for this theory. Embedded in rocks found on several continents, for example, are the fossilized remains of a primeval fern-like tree species,

Evening storm clouds approach a grazing kangaroo.

called *Glossopteris*. These trees are thought to have been part of a worldwide forest. There is no way, the theorists claim, that identical species could have arisen independently in what are today widely separated locations.

Anyway, about 225 million years ago Pangaea broke into two huge pieces. The two parts, Laurasia and its southern sister, Gondwana, slowly drifted away from each other. At this stage both pieces were considered supercontinents; Gondwana included land that would eventually become Antarctica, Africa, South America, India, Madagascar and Australia.

Gondwana lay near the South Pole and luxuriated in a much warmer climate than exists today at those latitudes. Then, some 150 million to 100 million years ago, Gondwana began to break up. Africa and India first departed, leaving Australia connected to South America and Antarctica. Around 40 million to 45 million years ago, Australia (with part of New Guinea on its leading edge) broke loose and began slowly drifting north. By about 15 million years ago (give or take a million) it had nearly reached its present position. It is still moving, however, by a centimeter or two annually.

Mammals Make Their Debut

All this breaking up and drifting around was very important for the evolution of mammals (and hence kangaroos). Mammals made their first appearance only slightly later than the reptiles. It is thought that all mammals descended from a mammal-like reptile some 220 million years ago. During that time two important and unique features were developed: hair for heat insulation and milk glands. These special milk glands called *mammae* (which give mammals their name) are used to feed the young.

Apparently the first mammals were rather small, shy critters that spent most of their time scuttling around in the underbrush chasing insects. Evolutionarily speaking, they didn't amount to much until after the dinosaurs lost ground. Only then did mammals evolve to become the dominant animal form on earth.

Mammals differ from reptiles in several other ways, especially when you are looking for fossils. Soft tissues, such as muscles, reproductive organs and hair hardly ever become preserved in rock. But hard parts such as bones or teeth often do. There are singular exceptions, though.

"Most of the early kangaroo fossils are very fragmentary, rarely consisting of more than parts of the skull," writes paleontologist and zoology professor Michael Archer of the University of New South Wales. "The most complete have been found in clays overlying the brown coal seams mined at Morwell in Victoria . . . Surprisingly, the grass in the stomach areas is still green. Impressions of skin, nails and mats of fur have been found and some skeletons even have the remains of tiny joeys preserved in the region of the pouch. . . ."

To a fossil hunter, one of the more important distinguishing characteristics of the mammalian skeleton is the lower jaw. In modern mammals it's made of only one bone, while in the reptiles (and fish) it consists of several. Teeth are a good clue, too. Reptile teeth are continuously replaced throughout life. Mammals have a maximum of only two sets—the milk teeth and the permanent teeth.

Mammals Begin Wearing Pouches

One of nature's hallmarks is diversity; rarely does anything stay the same for very long. After the first mammals appeared, their stocks split into two principal groups.

One band became the *protherians*, the egg-laying mammals, which evolved into such weird species as platypuses and echidnas, while the other group became the *therians*, characterized by having a placenta and giving birth to live young.

Some 50 million years later the therians split into two groups again. This division was again characterized by differences in reproductive strategy. The *eutherians* or "true placentals" had developed an approach in which the young spend a long period of time developing in an enlarged uterus attached to its wall by a placenta. The placenta obtains nutrients and oxygen by diffusion from the uterine wall and transports them to the growing embryo via an umbilical cord. When eutherian mammals are born, they are relatively large and often precocious and semi-independent of the mother (as in the case of gazelles). Humans, cats and rats are other examples of the placental way of life.

Marsupials, on the other hand, took a different tack. This group adopted very short pregnancies and gave birth to only partially formed young. While in the

Like all marsupials, kangaroos are characterized by having a pouch to raise their young in. This Common wallaroo mother cleans its baby's ears by licking them.

uterus, the embryo is nourished by mucous membrane secretions from the wall of its womb. Marsupials do not develop a placenta comparable to eutherians, utilizing instead a kind of simple "yolk-sac" arrangement. This method of obtaining nutrition is not very efficient and once the embryo has reached a certain size it must find another source of food.

Immediately following birth, the infant marsupial crawls to a special pouch in its mother's body. (The name, "marsupial," is derived from *marsupion*, the Greek word for pouch.) Here it stays, enclosed and protected, while it completes its development attached to one of its mother's milk nipples. To prevent it from falling off, the teat swells in the nursing baby's mouth.

Marsupials coexisted with dinosaurs some 85 million years ago. Their oldest fossils are found in North American deposits, where they are thought to have first evolved. New forms soon spread widely into South America (which was still linked to Australia and Antarctica) and it is from these South American animals that the Australian fauna was apparently derived.

Now comes a curious twist to the tale: Eutherian (placental) mammals apparently initially developed in Asia. They reached North America late in the Cretaceous Period, somewhere around 70 million years ago, when there was no sea barrier between the two land masses.

This invasion was followed by a major evolutionary explosion of new species that replaced most of the marsupials. Competition with the invading placentals is usually offered as the reason, but this was also the time when the dinosaurs finally died out. Whatever the explanation for these extinctions, though, few marsupials survived this period. The possums were among the most successful of the survivors; some eighty species exist today.

As waves of the new mammals spread into South America, the marsupials out on the "front lines" continued to make their way to the Australian end of Gondwana. When Australia finally broke away from Gondwana it carried a vanguard of marsupial mammals that had apparently "outrun" most of the eutherian invasion.

Safe on this continental raft, the marsupials blossomed into numerous forms to fill all of the available living spaces, from treetop to forest floor. One ancestral group, the diprodonts, small possum-like tree dwellers, would eventually give rise to the kangaroos and wallabies. ("Wallaby" is a loose term applied to any kangaroo species that weighs less than 45 pounds [20 kilograms] as an adult.)

There is evidence, however, that suggests marsupials are better adapted than placental mammals for life in unpredictable climates such as Australia's. In his paper, "Marsupial Origins: Taxonomic and Biological Considerations," J. Kirsch observes:

> In an unpredictable environment a placental female has no option but to continue to term, at which time the young still may be lost due to lactation failure if poor conditions persist. A considerable depletion of reproductive value will then have occurred.
>
> Marsupial females, on the other hand, uniformly have energetically cheap gestations; like placentals, they can terminate investment in the young at any time after birth, but birth occurs *before* substantial investment of resources has taken place.

This reproductive capacity may help explain why marsupials are usually among the first mammals to recover their populations after a serious climatic upset.

KANGAROOS BOUND INTO THE SCENE

The earliest fossil indications that kangaroos were going to appear on the Australian scene have tentatively been dated as 25 million years in age; 10 million years later, however, there were definitely living, breathing "primitive kangaroos" lurking about.

"The area was covered in a vast rainforest intersected by huge slow-flowing rivers and expansive lakes," says professor Archer. "Freshwater dolphins and crocodiles shared the waters, while the forests were inhabited by many kinds of marsupials."

The oldest kangaroo fossils known so far came from Tommo's Quarry on Lake Tarkarooloo in South Australia. The largest of these early kangaroos, when alive, would have weighed about 18 ounces (500 grams). It was probably a browsing animal and most likely bounded (using all four feet instead of hopping).

The Musky rat-kangaroo, which inhabits the rainforests of northeastern Australia, may be a kind of living portrait of those first kangaroos. This little kangaroo forages on the ground for a wide variety of foods, including insects, and when alarmed runs boundingly away. (We examine the rat-kangaroos in detail in chapter 4.)

No one is sure whether or not the earliest kangaroo was a tree-dweller or lived on the forest floor. But soon after its appearance (and disappearance) came kangaroo-like forms that did live on the ground. Hopping also developed sometime during this time. With locomotion now centered on the hind legs, the front paws were freed to become hands for manipulating food and for grooming. The prehensile tail, so helpful for hanging onto branches in the trees, now became a kind of counterbalance when hopping.

BIG CHANGES AND KANGAROO SURVIVALISTS

About 8 million years ago Australia began to experience some dramatic climate changes. The center of the continent was drying out; rainforests were giving way to open woods and grasslands. The old rainforest still exists, to a limited extent, on the northern and eastern margins of the continent. Spreading grassland seemed to prepare the stage for the rapid expansion of kangaroos, the most successful adapting marsupial in this new habitat.

Kangaroos gradually increased in size and changed their diet. Instead of just browsing on the leaves of trees and shrubs, some of the forest wallabies began eating grasses. Over time their teeth changed to cope with this coarser material and their stomachs became more complicated, forming sack-like fermentation chambers, in order to digest it.

The larger an animal is, the more grass it can process and the greater value it will get from a meal. According to Michael Archer, some modern-day species, such as the wallaroo (a mid-sized species of kangaroo), can accommodate up to one-eighth of its body weight in food. It needs such a large stomach because its fodder (like coarse Spinifex grass) is so poor in nutrition that it needs to eat huge quantities and hold it in its stomach for quite a long time to allow the resident micro-organisms to properly break down the cellulose. (Sheep and cattle also digest by fermentation.) As the prairies became more extensive and kangaroos began moving out of the forests to become grassland animals, they also became more social, often feeding and traveling together. In the past, their ancestors were small enough to hide in the forest undergrowth. When a predator discovered them, they would dash away with a surprisingly explosive leap. Because these new animals had no place to hide on the plains, they adopted the simple expedient of running away from all danger.

"Since flight works best with an effective early warning system," wrote John Vandenbeld in his book, *The Nature of Australia*, "the greater togetherness promoted by grazing became an advantage, with more eyes to detect danger."

The kangaroo's adaptations for survival seem to closely parallel those of the hooved animals on the grasslands of other continents. Perhaps it's the prairie itself that ultimately determines how an animal behaves and functions. Anyway, of all the distinctive types of marsupials in Australia, only kangaroos emerged dominant.

These clumps of Spinifex grass typify the nutritionally poor fodder that is generally available to grazing kangaroos in central Australia.

THE NEW GUINEA CONNECTION

When Australia, drifting on its northerly course, collided with the Asian continental plate some 15 million years ago, it formed the basis of the world's second largest island, New Guinea. This crash abruptly slowed Australia's northern movement and created New Guinea's highlands when the edges of the two plates crumpled upward. Rising to several thousand meters in altitude, these mountains continue to grow at a rate of about one-tenth of an inch ($^1/_4$ centimeter) per year.

Present-day Australia is separated from New Guinea only by the shallow (45-feet- [13-meters-] deep) Torres Strait. At various times in the past, when sea levels fell, there was a dry-land connection between Australia and New Guinea via this strait. This very important link allowed kangaroos to migrate back and forth from the mainland. Several species of wallabies and some closely related tree-kangaroo genera are now shared between the two landmasses.

Paleontologist Michael Archer displays a skull and jaw bone of a fossil kangaroo found at Riversleigh. The earliest kangaroo fossils are about 25 million years old.

This land bridge also allowed rodents to invade Australia. No one really knows how long they have been there or what havoc they created in competing with the smaller kangaroo species. However, they have been here long enough to have evolved a number of unique species. By the time of European discovery and settlement, rodents comprised almost a quarter of the mammal species living on the continent.

The Riversleigh Site

Scientists are only now discovering the variety and abundance of extinct fauna that once existed in Australia. Found on a remote homestead (called Riversleigh Station) in western Queensland, an impressive array of limestone-encrusted fossils is helping to shed new light on the evolution of life.

The first fossils discovered there in 1901 weren't studied seriously, but in 1963, American paleontologist Richard Tedford and Australian geologist Alan Lloyd went to Riversleigh and made an amazing collection of fossilized bones. Their work resulted in the identification of three new mammal species.

Every year since 1976, Michael Archer makes the long, difficult journey to Riversleigh to continue chipping at these rocks. Lately he has been joined by another scientist, Sue Hand.

"Millions of years ago this plateau was dense rainforest," Archer explains. "Like other continents, early Australia was populated by giants. Cow-sized marsupials and more than a dozen kinds of kangaroos browsed in the understory."

One of the more unusual animals to have lived here was a marsupial lion (*Thylacoleo carnifex*), which is believed to have preyed on kangaroos. Killing them on the ground, the lion may have dragged its victims up into trees for consumption, much the way leopards eat their prey today. This unique predator was equipped with grasping hands and was probably an excellent climber. Although they were widely scattered throughout Australia, they became extinct some 17,000 years ago during the big Pleistocene die-off.

Another remarkable animal found at Riversleigh is the giant short-faced kangaroo (*Procoptodon goliah*), the largest kangaroo known to have ever lived. Standing more than 10 feet (3 meters), it is estimated to have weighed as much as 650 pounds (300 kilograms).

Besides possessing a shortened, almost bulldog-like face, this species also had very long and unusual arms. "Each hand had two very long fingers with thin, straight claws and three much shorter fingers," Archer explains. "The two long claws may have acted as grappling hooks to bring foliage within reach." It too vanished, along with 13 or so other related short-faced species, in the Pleistocene epoch.

THE HOLOCAUST OF THE PLEISTOCENE

"The Pleistocene Epoch (from 2 million to 10,000 years ago) was a time of great change," continues Archer. "Extreme fluctuations in climate saw the growth and retreat of the great ice sheets at the Earth's poles, a phenomenon that was repeated many times. Sea level fell as water was locked away in polar ice, and then rose again as the ice melted."

Australian deserts grew well beyond their present extent, creating huge areas of windblown dune-fields in the continent's center. In the meantime, the higher mountains became covered by snow and glaciers. Many new kinds of kangaroos evolved in response to these conditions but many more became extinct.

The last part of the Pleistocene Epoch (about 10,000 to 20,000 years ago) saw the extinction of nearly all the large animals of Australia. For reasons that are unknown, mass extinction became a worldwide phenomenon during this time and occurred in Europe, Asia and North and South America as well. Some large kangaroo species that did not become extinct during this crisis apparently became reduced in size. The Eastern grey kangaroo, for example, may be a dwarfed descendant of the much larger *Macropus titan*. This extinct 330-pound (150-kilogram) kangaroo weighed twice as much as its living relatives.

THE ABORIGINE FACTOR

Mankind may have had a hand in some of the extinctions during the Pleistocene Epoch. Human beings can be extremely efficient hunters, even when armed with only primitive weapons like spears and pit-falls. People are also very selective, aiming for the biggest animals first. It doesn't take much effort to imagine the aftermath of constant "high-graded" hunting in a given area. In Australia there is direct evidence that Aboriginal occupation dates back at least 40,000 years and some researchers believe they have been there for perhaps as long as 120,000 years.

Tim Flannery, a biologist with the Australia Museum, maintains that extinctions don't correlate well with the ice ages or anything else climatic.

"There's a definite correlation between the arrival of human beings and the extinction of megafauna," he says. "Madagascar and New Zealand 1,000 years ago; North America about 11,000 years ago; Australia about 40,000 years ago. The results are devastating. In Australia nearly every native land mammal over about 150 pounds (70 kilograms) disappeared; the largest one left is the Red kangaroo."

Dr. Flannery is keenly interested in the fauna of New Guinea. This huge island consists of more than 311,000 square miles (807,000 square kilometers) of rough terrain and jungle. A few years ago, he discovered evidence of a new kind of tree-kangaroo living there. By the time he was able to examine a living specimen, however, native hunting pressure had all but forced the species into extinction. Of course, not everyone agrees with Dr. Flannery's overall assessment. Some critics express grave doubts about early humans being able to cause extinctions on a continental scale. On islands such as Madagascar or New Zealand it's possible, they allow. But on a land mass as big as Australia, the more likely culprit is severe climate change. Primitive humans, they insist, probably had little effect on healthy animal populations. Personally, I doubt if this last assertion is entirely true.

KANGAROO CLASSIFICATION

Taxonomy, the classification of animals by apparent physical and genetic similarities, is another subject often vigorously debated among biologists. Kangaroos, for example, were originally classified as rodents. Two hundred years later they were placed in the same family as possums. Recently, they have been given their own super-family, *Macropodoidae* (named after their common characteristic: large hind feet), to themselves but even this division seems unsatisfactory to some taxonomists.

It's generally agreed, though, that the kangaroo family tree has three main living branches: the Musky rat-kangaroo (a species out on a limb of its own); the bettongs and potoroos (the regular rat-kangaroos); and macropods, the so-called true kangaroos (which include all the wallabies and tree-kangaroos).

Depending upon which reference you believe, there are somewhere between 49 and 95 species of kangaroos in the world. This uncertainty reflects the generally unstable state of macropod taxonomy (and taxonomy in general). As new techniques, such as protein serology and DNA fingerprinting, are applied, the list of kangaroo species may grow substantially in the near future. At present, 57 recognized living species and six others recently thought to be extinct are listed in Appendix II of this book.

GENERAL DISTRIBUTION AND HABITATS

The kangaroo family is distributed generally throughout Australia (including Tasmania and some smaller offshore islands) and New Guinea. Approximately one-quarter of all kangaroo species (some 16 at present count) live in New Guinea.

About 8 million years ago, this central Australian region was covered with lush rainforests. Today's much drier climate supports mostly open woods and grassland.

Seventy percent of Australia has been classified as arid or semi-arid country. However, this doesn't mean the landscape is vacant of trees; scattered cover exists in all but the most barren desert areas. Much of Australia's woodlands are composed chiefly of eucalypts (more than 600 species have been identified). Everywhere they dominate the landscape, from wet coastal forest and dry sclerophyll timberland where the trees form a single-layer canopy with a grassy understory, to the mallee woods, which are stunted and multistemmed from the harsh conditions and frequent fires. The eucalyptus forests typically lead out into gullies and thickets and it's here that we often find rat-kangaroos and the smaller wallabies. In the border zone between forest and grassland, the larger wallabies and kangaroos hide in the shade by day and move out to feed on the grassy plains at night. Some of my most memorable moments have been sights of kangaroos hopping across a rosy plain toward tree cover at sunrise.

As in prehistoric times, today's rainforests remain an important environment for kangaroos. Although Australia's entire rainforest area technically covers a mere 0.3% of the country's total area, it is actually quite substantial. Queensland alone contains more than 3 million acres (1.2 million hectares) of this important habitat. Although the forests are fragmented and threatened by heavy logging, they still contain an astonishing number of plants and animal species including several rat-kangaroos, pademelons and hefty tree-kangaroos. Nearly 25 percent of Australia's rainforests are now protected in national parks.

The largest remaining rainforest habitat containing kangaroos is found in New Guinea. A few species are shared with Australia, but some of the most finely-adapted jungle-floor mammals—the dorcopsis wallabies—are exclusively New Guinean. To help avoid troublesome forest leeches, dorcopsis squats rather than sits, resting only the very tip of its tail on the ground. In this way, a minimum of surface area is available for a roving leech to latch onto.

Kangaroos are also found in steep, rocky areas and on open plains. Since Australian grasslands and deserts often have high air temperatures and prolonged drought, the kangaroos inhabiting these regions have developed special behaviors and metabolisms for surviving such an environment. One species, the Red kangaroo, is superbly adapted to these brutal conditions.

"Camels and kangaroos resemble each other in their cardiovascular response to dehydration," says Dr. Terry Dawson of the University of New South Wales. "When they lose water, they adjust the volume of the vascular system so that the functioning of the heart is not jeopardized. The kidney of the arid-zone kangaroo has concentrating abilities superior to those of comparable placental mammals."

Because of these and other adaptations, the water requirements of the Red kangaroo are about the same as those for a camel. According to Dawson's field studies, arid-zone kangaroos turn over only one-quarter of the water needed by sheep and wild goats. Many kangaroos obtain all their daily moisture needs from the plant material they eat and do not have to drink water unless there is a vegetation-withering drought. They can also survive a 20 percent weight loss of water without apparent harm.

As mentioned earlier, a number of offshore islands near Australia contain populations of macropods. These islands (technically called continental islands) were isolated from the mainland by either erosion or a rise in sea level (or both) sometime around 10,000 to 15,000 years ago.

Separated from the mainland, the kangaroos living on them became marooned. After a weeding-out process of what might be called natural selection, many of the island populations have developed unique strains of their own. Some kangaroo species, cut off from sources of fresh water, have even been able to adapt to a desert island life by eating seaweed and drinking salt water.

These small island populations have become extremely important to conservationists. As a plague of feral herbivores (rabbits, goats, pigs) and predators (foxes and cats) swept across the mainland with the European settlers, they decimated many populations of smaller kangaroos. Only the isolation of these continental islands offers continued hope for the survival of several endangered species.

Rottnest Island, off Australia's west coast near Perth, is one of these important islands. The island supports a large population of a small kangaroo called a Quokka (also known as the Short-tailed wallaby). Their somewhat rat-like appearance gave the island its name when in 1696 Dutch explorers mistook the abundant Quokkas for large rats and called the place "rottnest" (early Dutch for rat's nest) as they sailed away.

Today's Rottnest Island is a popular holiday resort offering sun, surf and sand. Quokkas are still common here, even though they generally have become rare on the mainland. A century ago they were abundant in nearly all the swampy areas that skirted the coast of southwestern Australia. During that time of plenty, Aborigines were able to kill great numbers of them for food. Now Quokkas are seldom seen except as cheeky panhandlers of food from the tourists of Rottnest.

The Quokka.

"Feral" 'Roos in Exotic Places

Soon after Australia was discovered by the western world, people began exporting kangaroos to countries around the globe. Some of the animals went to zoos, while others became pets or stock for private estates. Inevitably, a few animals escaped, reproduced and established new colonies in strange lands.

In 1916, several Brush-tailed rock-wallabies (*Petrogale penicillata*) that had been purchased from the zoo in Sydney, Australia, and were on their way to the U.S. mainland were accidentally released when dogs tore open their cage in Honolulu, Hawaii. A single pair survived the mauling. Because the island's rocky slopes provided a favorable habitat for the runaways, an independent population soon developed. Their numbers seem to fluctuate with drought conditions. In 1981 the colony contained nearly 250 animals but currently the population is estimated at somewhere between 80 and 100 individuals. Some wildlife biologists speculate that the decline of Hawaii's rock-wallaby population may also be due to inbreeding.

In Great Britain, two separate populations of Bennett's wallabies from Tasmania (*Macropus rufogriseus rufogriseus*, a subspecies of the Red-necked wallaby) have been reported. One colony, in the Peak District, was begun by five animals that escaped during the early years of World War II. These animals, capable of surviving England's worst winters, are now regarded by locals as being "almost native" animals. In another few hundred years they probably will be considered indigenous.

Kangaroos have also been successfully introduced into New Zealand. Since the turn of the century, five species of wallabies have become so well established that New Zealand may have nearly as many wallabies today as does Australia.

In one exceptional case, the Parma wallaby (*Macropus parma*), believed to be extinct by the 1930s on the mainland, was found in large numbers on tiny Kawau Island, near Auckland, New Zealand.

Sir George Grey, an early explorer of Australia who eventually became governor of New Zealand, had a country estate on Kawau Island in the 1870s. During his many visits to Australia, he brought back several species of wallabies—which he released on the grounds. The Parmas flourished. In 1965, at the time they were rediscovered, it was reported that local farmers were actually shooting them as pests.

A number of Parmas were trapped for shipment, breeding and ultimate repatriation back on the mainland. Two years later, however, an indigenous group was discovered in the state forests in the Watagan Mountains of New South Wales. Since then, more small populations have been found in the forested areas of coastal New South Wales. Although they may seem locally common, conservation officials warn, Parma wallabies are still considered rare.

MIAs (Missing in Australia)

A species is generally considered extinct if it has not been seen alive in the past 50 years. In the last 200 years, Australia has witnessed some 17 mammal species become extinct (out of a total of 36 mammal extinctions worldwide).

Some species became threatened after land-clearing by farmers and grazing stock seriously changed their habitat. A few of these species were seriously in decline even before Europeans began to settle in Australia; civilization and competition from introduced predators simply speeded up the process.

The smaller kangaroos were most severely affected; six species are now thought to be extinct, while another seven or eight species are considered endangered. (A complete listing of the conservation status of all kangaroo species can be found in Appendix II.)

Hunting may have also been an important factor in the extinction of some species. The Toolache wallaby (*Macropus greyi*), for example, was common until the early 1900s in the nearly treeless long-grass and sedge country of southeastern South Australia. Because it had an exceptionally beautiful pelt and was very fast, the Toolache was a popular quarry for hunters. The open terrain allowed horses to be used in the chase and coursing events were held regularly. By the 1920s, however, the species had become restricted to a very tiny range.

"Concerned people of the time tried to remove some of the survivors on Konetta Sheep Run to a sanctuary on Kangaroo Island," writes Professor Archer. "But because they used dogs to chase the animals, only four dead and dying animals were obtained. Ironically, it was probably this solitary gesture of concern by Europeans that caused the final demise of the species."

No specimens of Toolache wallaby have been obtained since 1924 but unconfirmed sightings are occasionally reported.

Local extinctions due to habitat degradation and livestock competition is one of modern wildlife management's greatest miseries. When an area begins to lose its species diversity, it is evident that our conservation plans have been terribly inadequate.

One Australian region that is particularly troubled is the Riverina, a sort of plains country sandwiched between the Murray and Murrumbidgee rivers in southern New South Wales. It's long been known as extremely good pasture country so the problem is not obvious to everyone.

"In the 1850s, when the early explorers went through, something like 50-odd species of marsupials lived here," says Bill Poole, a biologist with the CSIRO (Commonwealth Scientific and Industrial Research Organisation). "Today there's only about three or four (species). This extreme loss comes mostly from habitat changes and competition resulting from the introduction of sheep. Many of those marsupials which disappeared were grass-dwelling . . . and were also affected by competition from rabbits and predation by foxes."

Rabbits, which were introduced into Australia in 1859 by Victorian settler Thomas Austin, may have played a decisive role in the rarity or extinction of some small kangaroo species that live in the inland deserts, beyond the range of grazing stock. Although rabbits are generally rare in desert areas, they quickly become very abundant following a season with adequate rain. Besides competing for food, they may physically displace kangaroos. Australia's only underground kangaroo, the Burrowing bettong (*Bettongia lesueur*), sometimes has its warrens usurped by invading rabbits. This species no longer occurs on the mainland and is currently restricted to a few small coastal islands.

RARE DISCOVERIES

Apparent rarity, however, is sometimes misleading. Some of the early explorers who traversed much of the continent during the first half of the 19th century commented in their journals about the singular lack of mammal sightings. A few of them starved as a result. Wild mammals were important food items to those expeditions.

Does this mean that kangaroos and other mammals were generally rare before the settlement of Australia by Europeans? I doubt it. It's more likely that those explorers were in poor kangaroo territory or simply not aware of some of the smaller nocturnal species inhabiting the area. Mammals can be exceedingly wary and seem scarce, especially in a country as big and varied as Australia. In fact, nearly one-fifth of this continent's 224 mammal species have only been seen a few times.

After a thorough field investigation, as in the case of the Parma wallaby, wild mammals are occasionally found to be much more common in some areas than they were originally thought to be. Sometimes these studies even lead to the discovery of new and unsuspected species. During the early 1980s, the existence of two unique kangaroos species, the Long-footed potoroo (*Potorous longipes*) and the Proserpine rock-wallaby (*Petrogale persephone*) was revealed.

Another phenomena concerning rare Australian animals is that they seem to turn up in increasing numbers after there are a long series of droughts. Says Professor

Some kangaroos, such as this Red kangaroo, have been able to take advantage of lands overgrazed by domestic stock. However, in order to survive in large numbers, these big kangaroos often rely on wells and other man-made watering points.

Archer, "I think the reason is that the drought clobbers the competing introduced animals first. They can't cope where the native Australian animals can."

From a conservationist's point of view, Archer feels that a decade-long run of droughts in Australia might eliminate introduced animals from that continent's arid center. "Perhaps this would give the smaller native fauna a chance to bounce back," he says hopefully. "It's the small things, the 'ankle-biters' [not the big kangaroos] that suffer so badly when conditions get good and introduced animal populations begin to build up."

Not every scientist agrees with this view, however. Dr. Gerry Maynes of the Australian National Parks and Wildlife Service contends that the idea of a severe drought aiding the recovery of a native species is probably a forlorn hope.

"During a drought, all animals are forced back onto the dwindling resources available before populations crash," he says. "Small species are more likely to lose out due to their limited ability to range widely for food."

CIVILIZED BENEFITS FOR KANGAROOS

It may be a mistake to assume that all developments from civilization have been to the detriment of kangaroos. Some of the larger species, such as the Red and Grey kangaroos, have greatly expanded their numbers and range in the last 200 years. The most widely held reason is the increased supply of available water. Throughout Australia's interior region are numerous wells, bored deep into the ground to tap the waters of the Great Artesian Basin.

Water from these bores and the many earthen storage tanks built to provide drinking water for domestic stock have enabled kangaroos to survive in places normally uninhabitable during droughts. Because of their greater mobility, kangaroos are better able to take advantage of these artificial watering points than the domestic stock that they were built for. After several good seasons with this steady water supply, kangaroo populations can expand to incredible numbers. Food then becomes the limiting factor.

Other, more subtle, reasons for the general build-up in kangaroo numbers also exist. Some observers point to the control of their predators, the Dingo (Australia's wild dog) and the Aborigine, as an important factor. Countering that idea, though, is a growing realization that land overgrazed by sheep is often ideal kangaroo habitat. (See chapter 7 for a complete discussion of these issues.)

DROUGHT AND POPULATION TRENDS

Rainfall and drought are considered the most significant agents of short-term change in population density. During a severe drought, up to 70 percent of the kangaroos in a given region have been known to die.

To increase their chances for survival, the larger kangaroo species move further in their search for food and water. (Normally they don't stray more than 6 or 9 miles [10 or 15 kilometers] from a water source.) Other species like the Euro or Common wallaroo (*Macropus robustus*) and some of the smaller wallabies are physiologically adapted to arid conditions and tend to stay in one area near known food and water reserves. Large die-offs will occur, though, should those resources completely fail during a prolonged drought.

When the drought does finally break and good weather prevails, lost members of the population are quickly replaced. Under ideal conditions, some species may increase their numbers by more than 40 percent annually.

Aging and Kangaroo Teeth

All kangaroos have the same general tooth pattern (dentition). Located in the front part of the upper jaw are six incisors, which form a crescent-shaped cutting edge. The lower jaw contains only two, but significantly larger, incisors, which rest behind the upper incisors and cut against them when feeding. The grinding teeth, or molars, are situated in the back of the mouth on both sides of the upper and lower jaws.

There is a long gap between the incisors and molars. This space evidently provides room for the animal's tongue, which helps arrange grasses and other cut herbage before passing them back for chewing, and is quite useful for kangaroos and wallabies with a grazing or browsing diet. Rat-kangaroos, on the other hand, have the same general dentition but their individual teeth are adapted for a more omnivorous diet, which may include mushrooms and insects. The incisors are more pointed and the molars seem better designed for shearing or cutting rather than crushing tough plant material.

Another feature of kangaroo teeth is that the molars erupt in slow succession over a long period of time. As the animal matures, these teeth move in a predictable sequence forward along the jaw and eventually fall out. A method of determining the age of kangaroos has been developed by scientists. The method compares the degree of molar progression to an index for that species. An animal in full maturity, for example, will have a full complement of four molars on each side of the upper and lower jaws. A younger one may have only the first two molars in use, while a very old kangaroo might be using no more than the last one or two molars left in the series. In the wild, the life expectancy of Red and Grey kangaroos is about 15 to 18 years; less for the smaller species.

Sequential replacement of its molars permits a kangaroo to cope with very abrasive food, such as grasses and certain leaves. Instead of wearing down an entire

Kangaroos range greatly in size. The largest is the Red kangaroo (on the left) while the Long-nosed potoroo skull (on the right) represents one of the smallest species. A Red-necked wallaby skull (in the middle) represents the approximate mid-range in size. Notice how the incisor teeth are designed for nipping plant material.

set evenly, new teeth are successively brought into use. (Elephants also have serial molar replacement.)

The Nabarlek (*Petrogale concinna*), a small rock-wallaby found in extreme northern Australia, is the notable macropod exception to this phenomenon. Its molars continue to erupt, move forward and be shed throughout life. Nabarleks are known to seek food plants that contain higher silica contents than do other kangaroos. One fern species that is regularly consumed by them contains as much as 26 percent silica. The Nabarlek's super-abrasive diet probably led to the development of its unique molar replacement system.

DIETS AND DIGESTION

Body size is the key element in understanding the variation in macropod diets. The small species, such as bettongs and rat-kangaroos, are all somewhat omnivorous but tend to rely heavily on certain high-quality foods such as underground fungi. The medium-sized kangaroos (wallabies) utilize a mixture of browsing and grazing strategies to consume a wide variety of leafy vegetation. They characteristically choose food with a relatively low fiber content. The larger kangaroos are true grazers and specialize in eating grass.

Cellulose, the principal carbohydrate in grass, is an important part of all plant tissue. It forms the basis of every cell wall. Since no mammal can synthesize the enzymes needed to break down cellulose, symbiotic associations between certain mammals and bacteria or protozoa that have such enzymes have evolved. These micro-organisms live in the animal's gut and, by a fermentation process, release the nutrients bound in cellulose.

Fermentation digesters "house" their micro-organisms in special sections of the digestive system. In horses and rabbits, they live in parts of the hind gut such as the caecum. In kangaroos and ruminants, like cattle and sheep, the enlarged sections of the esophagus, stomach and upper parts of the small intestine act as the fermentation chambers.

All macropods are able to digest by fermentation to some degree; rat-kangaroos less so than the large grass-eating plains kangaroos, which have extremely well-developed fermentation systems. These kangaroos are able to exploit the high-fiber, low-nutritional environments of Australia's arid interior.

The end products of fermentation are mostly fatty-acids that are absorbed into the bloodstream and transformed by the liver into glucose. The fermenting micro-organisms also allow nitrogen to be recycled, thus conserving this valuable nutrient when food intake is low in nitrogen.

"Urea, formed by the breakdown of protein in the body, is returned in the saliva to the forestomach," says kangaroo physiologist Terry Dawson. "Here it is resynthesized into nutritive protein by the resident bacteria instead of being entirely excreted in the urine and lost. This recycling helps to conserve body water that otherwise would be needed for more frequent urination."

Kangaroos possess kidneys that are extremely good at concentrating what little urine is actually eliminated.

Occasionally, while watching a kangaroo feed or at rest, it will throw its head back and make a series of violent heaving movements of the chest and abdomen. It is regurgitating food, which is then briefly chewed and reswallowed. Sometimes a green liquid trickles out of its mouth during rechewing.

Nearly all the macropods cough up partially chewed food and send it to the stomach once more; Rufous rat-kangaroos drop the regurgitated material onto the ground before re-eating it. Although kangaroos don't ruminate in the true sense, like cattle, they do seem to need to send at least part of their food around a couple of times. It might be that they are mixing it with extra saliva for use in the fermentation chamber, but I don't think anyone really understands this process completely.

Before digestion, the food is well chewed but, unlike sheep, it is not so finely ground as to destroy most of the seeds that have been ingested. This allows kangaroo fecal pellets to act as important seed stores during drought periods.

Most kangaroo guts also contain a variety of roundworms in the strongaloid family. All of the more than 200 stomachs of five species of kangaroos that I once examined contained worms in varying amounts and sizes. Sometimes the gut mass will contain up to 30 or 40 percent worms but even very heavy worm-loads do not seem to debilitate the animals in any noticeable way. It's quite possible that these worms are actually assisting in digestion by secreting important enzymes. If this is true, then they cannot be considered true parasites.

Kangaroos often lick their forearms when they are overheated. A dense network of capillaries located beneath this site functions as an efficient heat-exchanger.

Basic Metabolism and Keeping Cool

A study in which heart-rate transmitters were surgically implanted in kangaroos showed that the energetic costs associated with survival were roughly two-thirds that of similar-sized placental mammals. In other words, kangaroos have a metabolic rate far below that of a human or a sheep. As would be expected, the kangaroo's body temperature is also slightly lower, 96° to 98° Fahrenheit (35.5° to 36.7° Centigrade).

To stay cool on hot days, kangaroos pant, sweat and lick their arms. There is a dense capillary network inside the forearm beneath the site where they lick that acts as an efficient heat-exchanger when the saliva evaporates. Many smaller kangaroos, such as rat-kangaroos, also have profuse sweat glands in their tails.

Hopping is a surprisingly efficient method of locomotion. The hopping movement activates a kind of internal "visceral piston," which pumps air in and out of the lungs, thus saving on muscle effort.

HOPPING AND OTHER LOCOMOTIONS

As mentioned earlier in this chapter, members of the kangaroo family are called macropods because of their two large feet designed for efficient hopping. To be more precise, they hop on their enlarged fourth toe (and to a lesser degree on their fifth toe). The first toe has almost completely disappeared, while the inner second and third toes have fused together (the syndactyl claw) to form a fur grooming comb. When hopping, the kangaroo uses its tail as a counterbalance to its upper body, which pivots on the large spring-like hind legs. The up-and-down action of the tail of a hopping kangaroo looks a lot like an old-fashioned pump handle being worked. The hopping motion also activates a kind of internal "visceral piston," which pumps air in and out of the lungs, thus saving on muscle effort.

Although it is very helpful, the tail is not essential for hopping. In 1969, Australian biologists reported seeing a wild Grey kangaroo that hopped almost normally despite having lost all but six inches (15 centimeters) of its tail.

The largest kangaroos (the Reds) cruise somewhere between 15 to 20 miles per hour (24 to 32 kilometers per hour). At these speeds, a kangaroo hops far more efficiently than an animal running the same speed on four legs. In fact, because of the elastic storage of energy in its tendons, a hopping kangaroo continues to use less energy as its speed increases.

"Energy can be stored in such elastic fibrous tissues much as it is stored in the spring of a pogo stick," says Terry Dawson. "The Achilles tendon in a 40-kilogram [88-pound] animal is extremely large and is approximately 1.5 centimeters [0.6 of an inch] in diameter and about 35 centimeters [14 inches] long. The two broad sheets of tendons running inside the tail may also play a role in the elastic storage of hopping energy."

Within normal ranges, kangaroos increase their speed by increasing their stride length, not their hopping frequency.

"I've chased kangaroos along a fence-line up to about 35 kilometers per hour [22 miles per hour] without their changing hopping frequency," Dr. Dawson told me. "But once they get over about 35 Ks, their hopping frequency starts to go up. They don't like to go this fast and they do it in a real burst, which sends their energy [oxygen] consumption right up.

"The fastest I've been able to chase them is 50 kilometers per hour [31 miles per hour] and at that stage a medium-sized female Red kangaroo's stride length was just under six meters [19.5 feet]."

Above cruising speeds, though, the energy costs start rising. In an emergency, a Red kangaroo has been known to accelerate to more than 40 miles per hour (65 kilometers per hour) for a few hundred yards but it cannot maintain those speeds for very long.

When moving slowly, as in grazing or browsing, most kangaroos switch to another gait, the pentapedal or "crawl" walk. The animal travels in a sort of standing crouch with both forefeet on the ground, while the tail becomes a "fifth leg" that helps support the body when the large hind legs are swung forward together.

Those big legs have other uses too. Most kangaroo species thump the ground with their feet when alarmed or in danger, similar to the alarm signal given by rabbits. This signal, usually made by a fleeing macropod, is quite loud and probably alerts other animals over a considerable distance.

Kangaroos can also swim while kicking their hind legs alternately. (Contrary to a widespread belief, they can move their hind legs independently.)

"They swim very well, though they don't normally do so unless they absolutely have to," says Jeoff Ross, curator of mammals at Sydney's Taronga Zoo. "I've seen them cross streams when they were fleeing from a bush fire."

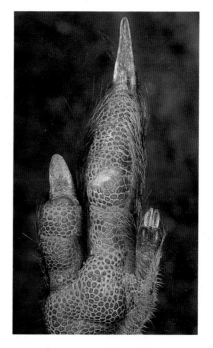

Kangaroos primarily hop on their enlarged fourth toe (the long middle digit). The first toe has almost completely disappeared, while the second and third toes have fused together to form a fur-grooming comb (small digit on right).

The "crawl walk" is used when a kangaroo is grazing or moving about slowly.

Agile wallabies on Stradbroke Island off Queensland's Gold Coast are also occasionally seen swimming the half-mile-wide channel to the mainland. Perhaps the proverbial grass is greener on the other shore.

Bio-bits and Pieces

At 7:00 A.M., New Year's Day, almost two years ago, I rolled up my sleeves and began dissecting a Swamp wallaby near Rosslyn Bay on the Queensland coast. I had planned to go to town that morning for a holiday breakfast but a fresh road-kill took precedence over my gastronomic intentions.

During the previous several days, as I drove toward Cooktown in northern Queensland, I had been watching the roadsides for a "just-road-killed" kangaroo. Like many highways in Australia, this avenue was littered with luckless wildlife that had been hit by passing vehicles. Unfortunately, the weather was very hot and an animal that was dead only a couple of hours would be too "ripe" for me to tolerate its dissection. After having stopped to investigate at least two dozen

carcasses along the way, a wallaby was hit by the car in front of me. Slipping it into a large plastic bag, I knew I had to work fast. The day was already heating up.

I'm not fond of blood and gore, but this session revealed some things about kangaroos that textbooks and live observation just can't do. I could leisurely examine its long jaws and the way the teeth fit in the mouth. After opening the chest, I found that only the upper one-third of the body (the narrowest part of the chest) contains the pericardial/lung cavity. I was also surprised to learn that kangaroos have very large hearts relative to their body size, when compared to other mammal species.

A creature is much more than the sum of its parts, though. I remember that maxim every time I see a kangaroo bounding effortlessly over a fence or rival males in fierce battle, or during the little quiet moments when youngsters are allowed to pull their mother's long ears.

A Swamp wallaby *forages on the succulent leaves of a tree's lower branches.*

LIFE IN THE POUCH:

Joey Grows Up

It was nearly sundown by the time we found the little green meadow we had heard about. Hoping to witness the interactions of a large group of kangaroos, Mark Newman and I had spent more than three days searching for this spot. It was here in the evening light that close to a hundred kangaroos, adults and young, might be seen together.

A month or so earlier a shallow pond had existed here, but a searing Australian drought had reduced it to slightly damp earth. The native grasses, taking advantage of this temporary bonanza of moisture, had grown quickly to set seed before they too became as brown and crisp as the surrounding country. Except for this temporary meadow, the only relief to the nearly flat landscape was a thin veneer of brittle, grey-colored bushes.

From a distance we could see numerous dark shapes moving across the lighter green of the grassy spot. Ever mindful of the failing light, we half-stalked, half-hurried toward them with our binoculars and camera gear. Stopping to set up our equipment behind a large shrub, we became spellbound as we watched more than two dozen kangaroos feed and play in the area just in front of us.

They were aware of our presence because now and then one would stand up and stare in our direction for a few moments before dropping back down on all fours to continue grazing. There was little to fear from us, though, for we were in a national park where hunting is banned.

Because undisturbed animals tend to spend a great deal of time resting in what little shade they can find during the heat of the Australian day, kangaroo watching can get a bit tedious. This group, though, seemed to be making up for an extra hot day. There was action everywhere we looked. A serious fight erupted between two large adult male Red kangaroos, while nearby, a female nearing oestrus (the short time when she is fertile) pretended indifference to an eagerly following third. After the fight ended, some of the younger animals began play-boxing with others their age, while others simply kicked up their heels and gamboled around their mothers.

One youngster, still in the pouch, stretched himself out as far as he could reach to nibble choice tidbits each time his mother got down to graze. On one occasion he reached too far and tumbled out of the pouch and onto the ground with a surprised "thump." This may have been the first time he had been out of his mother's pouch, because it took several tries before he could get his legs coordinated enough to stand and execute a couple of wobbly hops.

Immediately, several of the adults, including a huge male, began showing an interest in the little joey. (A baby kangaroo is called a "joey" from birth until it

Above: A group of young Eastern grey kangaroos gathers at sunset.

Opposite: A curious joey peers cautiously from its mother's pouch.

permanently vacates the pouch.) One at a time, they came over and sniffed its head. The big male pushed it with a forepaw, causing it to fall over. At this point the mother intervened, covering the youngster with her body and relaxing her pouch muscles to allow the opening to droop open. In a flash, the joey tumbled in. He'd had enough adventures for a while!

MISTAKEN IDEAS

The marsupial way of life has often been misinterpreted through the ages. Stranded Dutch navigator Francisco Pelsaert is credited with making some of the first observations about kangaroo reproduction, but he was misled by the minuteness of the pouch-embryos and their firm attachment to the nipple. He erroneously came to the conclusion that ". . . it seems certain that they grow there out of the nipples of the mammae, from which they draw their food."

Among the early depictions of kangaroos, I remember seeing one painting that showed four joeys sitting in a row in the mother's pouch. The artist must have assumed that since there were four teats in the pouch, there ought to be four babies. We know now that only one baby normally attaches itself to a teat and occupies the pouch. But every rule has its exceptions; the Musky rat-kangaroo, for example, commonly gives birth to twins.

In rare instances, individual females of other kangaroo species have been found carrying two young. Jack Higgins, longtime caretaker of Pebbly Beach Campground located on the coast south of Sydney, well known for its tame free-ranging kangaroos, once watched an Eastern grey kangaroo raise a set of twins.

"She got to the point where she couldn't carry the two," Higgins told me. "A fight would erupt between them whenever they both tried to get back in the pouch. Only one could get in; the other youngster being forced to follow along outside. But as soon as the one in the pouch came out, zip!, in went the other one. They kept swapping like this until Mum said, 'That's enough!' Then she wouldn't let either one of them back in. You know, I've lived here for more than 20 years and that's the first time I've ever seen twin 'roos."

Another early misconception asserted that the kangaroo's pouch was actually the uterus and semen is placed there by the male in order to fertilize the young. Careful observation eventually debunked this notion. In 1830, an English surgeon named Alexander Collie watched a captured Tammar wallaby give birth aboard his ship, H.M.S. *Sulpher*, which was anchored in Cockburn Sound near the present-day port of Fremantle. His account, published in the *Zoological Journal* of London, describes the diminutive infant's emergence at the cloaca and its unaided climb to the pouch opening. The mother, ". . . with her head turned towards her tender offspring seemed to watch its progress, which was about as expeditious as a snail."

Over the years since Dr. Collie's time, many of the details of kangaroo reproduction have been worked out. Each species has its own unique habits and timing but they all follow a general pattern, beginning with finding a mate.

MALES AND FEMALES: SOME PHYSICAL DIFFERENCES

While many other marsupials, such as koalas and wombats, have pouches that open towards the rear of the animal, all kangaroo pouches open forward to prevent

The adult male of each species of kangaroo is usually considerably larger than a female of the same age.

dumping the baby on the ground when the mother is hopping. Only the female possesses a pouch.

The inside of the pouch is warm and bare of fur. There are, however, a few coarse hairs located mostly around the teats. A protective layer of fur on the outside of the pouch, combined with a rich blood supply, help keep its temperature a cozy 90° Fahrenheit (32° Centigrade). The pouch contains four teats.

A kangaroo has a lot of muscle control over her pouch. She can relax the opening to let her joey out. If she is frightened, she can shrink the opening down to almost nothing in order to keep him in. I've heard stories of mother kangaroos carrying small "pouch young" being chased into water and swimming to the other side without drowning their babies. Larger joeys are usually lost because the pouch cannot form an effective seal around them. They also need more oxygen in order to survive.

Males of the larger kangaroo species develop massive biceps and forearms when they reach breeding age.

Internally, the female's two uteruses (all marsupials have two uteruses) join into the vagina, which is divided into three canals. In most species of kangaroos the young are born through the middle, or median, vagina. Just prior to the infant's leaving the body, all the vaginas become fused together, forming a single cavity. At this point, the urethra, the urine duct that comes from the bladder, joins in and creates a common urogenital sinus out of the lower vagina. Both the urogenital sinus and the rectum then open into another common sac, the cloaca, whose single opening to the outside world can be closed by a circular sphincter muscle.

The male also has a cloaca but his penis is not situated within it. It is separated by a fold of skin called the penis sac. The scrotum, containing his testicles, is positioned exterior and hangs on a cord-like muscle that can shorten to hold the testes close to the body during fights, cold weather or when hopping. When relaxed during peaceful times or warm temperatures, the scrotum may lengthen and drop 2 or 3 inches (5 or 8 centimeters).

Kangaroos exhibit a great deal of physical difference between the sexes, especially in size. Males may have body weights up to three times those of females.

COURTSHIP AND MATING

As the breeding cycle begins, male kangaroos show an increased interest in females and often follow them around, periodically sniffing their genital area. This sniffing may begin up to two days before oestrus and it lets the male know precisely when

A male Eastern grey kangaroo mates with a female while her young-at-foot joey stays nearby.

a female is ready to mate. Many kangaroo species are known as "continuous-breeders" and do not have a marked seasonality to their breeding cycle. However, every female must be in heat (oestrus) in order to be fertile and she may only be receptive for a few hours. To successfully mate, any hopeful male must be there at the right moment.

Some of the larger species, such as the Grey kangaroos and the Whiptail wallaby, seem to have a dominance hierarchy among the males in the group. This effectively reserves all mating rights to a single dominant male. Although no male kangaroo has been observed defending females and young from predators, they will defend their dominance (and consequently their mating rights) with other males. Occasionally, a furious fight may erupt between the dominant male and a rival that is nearly equal in his size and strength. A new dominant male may be the result. More often, the dominant male is replaced only when he dies. To keep the gene pool stirred up, however, subordinate males occasionally manage a "sneaky mating" or two when the "boss" is not looking.

The dominance factor may actually be an overrated idea. Recent studies carried out by Graeme Moss at the University of New South Wales's Arid Zone Research Station at Fowler's Gap, shows that the most reproductively active males (at least with Red kangaroos) may not necessarily be the biggest. The most successful breeding males seem to be those that live in areas with the highest densities of females. As oestrus nears, a female may even "advertise" herself to the neighborhood males by increasing her range of daily travel.

A courting male may stroke the female's tail, chest or neck as a kind of foreplay, his long tapered penis often erect in eager pursuit. Occasionally, he'll make a soft clucking sound as he gently scratches the base of her tail or lays a forepaw on her shoulder. Males of some smaller species are more assertive, moving the female's tail from side to side while periodically cuffing her. As their sexual excitement increases, one or both of the animals may sinuously lash its tail back and forth.

Head bobbing is another frequent component of courtship behavior with some wallaby species. Here, the male stands upright in front of the female and swings his head up and down or from side to side. Occasionally, he may attempt to block her progress.

The female usually moves away from these advances, often making a coughing or hissing sound to signal her annoyance. Although the male may attempt with increasing frequency to mate with her, she will rarely submit to mounting until oestrus has actually occurred. Rebuffed and frustrated, some males may temporarily relieve their tension by performing an aggressive grass-pulling display. They have also been known to masturbate.

The females of most species of kangaroos give birth a day or two before oestrus occurs. There are exceptions, such as the Swamp wallaby, which appears to mate just before the birth is due.

During actual mating, the male grasps the female around the lower abdomen and inserts his penis alongside her tail into the urogenital opening. The female usually has both forefeet on the ground and her hindquarters raised. Copulation may be as short as two minutes (for potoroos and Parma wallabies) or as long as 40 to 50 minutes (for Eastern grey kangaroos). Multiple ejaculations are common.

Males of some species, including Matchies tree-kangaroo and the Common wallaroo, leave behind a semen plug in the vagina after mating. Little understood, these interesting plugs of coagulated seminal fluid apparently prevent further mating by other males. In evolutionary terms, this is a nice strategy to insure that only one male's sperm will be available for fertilization after a mating. Semen plugs have also been found in animals as varied as Tasmanian devils, Springhaas and Viscachas.

Although its timing can be quite varied and complicated, kangaroo reproduction can be reduced to these basic events: The big joey is expelled from the pouch. He is allowed to drink milk from a teat but not to re-enter the pouch. (Some species continue to suckle for another four months.) The mother then gives birth 21 to 31 days after, depending upon the species. The new youngster crawls up into the pouch and firmly attaches itself to a teat. Then the female mates again. (Some species mate immediately following postpartum, others when the youngster is a bit older.)

Sometimes the whole sequence of events is compressed into one day (or night). Dr. Randy Rose of the University of Tasmania has studied the reproductive biology of bettongs, a group of small rat-like kangaroos. "The night the bettong youngster leaves the pouch is the same night that the new baby is born," Dr. Rose told me. "Accordingly, there is a precise mechanism that operates to see that the pouch is vacated before the birth. Otherwise, the larger young would trample the newborn in the pouch and kill it. The pouch contracts so strongly the night before the new baby is born that the larger youngster is unable to get back in. It's so tight, in fact, that he can't even stick his head in to get a drink of milk. However (and this is unusual), the pouch shuts around a protruding teat allowing him to still suckle. After giving birth, the mother then mates again (also during the same night)."

A BABY ON HOLD

Since the mother kangaroo already has a newborn baby in her pouch, why does she mate so soon? It's a complex strategy of assuring reproductive success: The fertilized egg develops to about the 100-cell stage and then becomes dormant. About the size of a pinhead, the tiny embryo's growth remains suspended until the present joey nears the end of its pouch life. (In the Red kangaroo, the embryo is dormant for about 200 days.) Reactivated, presumably by hormones, it then completes its development in time for the "weaning" and oestrus. Following a typical mating, a female may have, simultaneously, a quiescent embryo, a newly born pouch young and a still-nursing young-at-foot.

This process, called embryonic diapause, also assures that there is a fertilized embryo on hand to replace a pouch young that dies through accident or due to lack of sufficient milk during a drought. In this case, the embryo's development is reactivated when the stimulus from the suckling young is lost. In a prolonged drought, the young in the pouch die in progressively earlier stages until the female stops breeding altogether or the environment improves.

In normal circumstances, however, the adult females of most species of macropods are constantly pregnant. (The exceptions are the Musky rat-kangaroo and possibly the Western grey kangaroo.) A seasonal diapause has also been detected in kangaroos, such as Tammar and Bennett's wallabies, which live in areas having a very cold winter or other annual climatic extremes.

A good example of coping with a harsh climate may be the Quokkas of Rottnest Island, off Western Australia. Mainland Quokkas breed all year long, but on Rottnest they restrict their breeding time to the period from January to June. This is the hottest and driest time of the year and breeding Quokkas are in a semistarved state. By August and September, when nursing joeys are imposing their maximum stress on their mothers' bodies, the climate and forage conditions are at their best. It is interesting to note that after two years in captivity on an adequate diet, Rottnest Island Quokkas breed all year long.

Despite these characteristics, the maximum reproductive rate for most species of macropods is only two or three young per year. The normal birth interval for Red kangaroos, for example, is around eight months. Adverse climatic conditions may speed up the birthrate but it also delays the rate of weaned young. In a severe drought as much as 70 percent of a kangaroo population may die and most surviving adults will cease to breed. But they respond within days of drought-break-

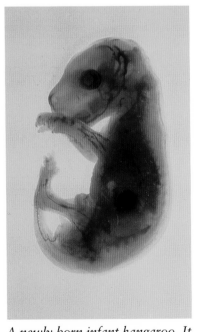

A newly born infant kangaroo. It is barely the size of a bean and only about .026 ounce (.75 gram).

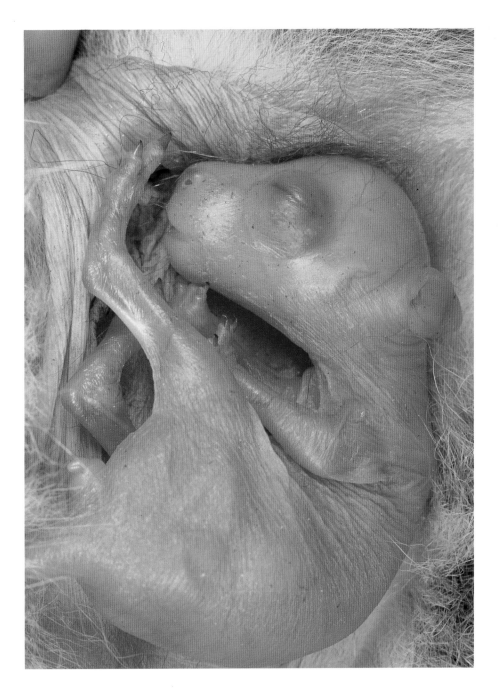

Firmly attached to a teat, a young Tammar wallaby grows quickly in the warm protection of its mother's pouch.

ing rains by beginning to mate again. With an annual growth rate of about 40 percent, most populations can return to normal within a year or two.

The actual gestation periods for embryonic growth ranges from 21 to 38 days, depending upon species. The potoroos have the shortest gestational length, while the bettongs seem to have the longest. The average for most of the kangaroo tribe is about 32 days.

BIRTH: THE BLESSED EVENT

There are no external signs that a kangaroo is pregnant. One of the first indications of approaching delivery is intensive pouch cleaning activity by the expecting female. For most of the gestation period, the skin inside the pouch has been secreting a brown waxy substance, which dries to a dark brown scale. Holding the pouch open with her forepaws, she nibbles at the crusty scale and then licks it away.

She then adopts the birth position, a typical posture for most kangaroo species. Supporting her back against a tree or other object, she sits heavily on the base of her tail, which extends forward between her hind legs. The hips are rotated so that the vulva points upwards and the upper torso is hunched forward over it. She licks the urogenital opening frequently.

About a half a minute or so before birth, a small amount (1 to 2 milliliters) of viscous yellow-colored yolk sac fluid appears at the opening. Occasionally it is tinged with blood. It is usually followed by an embryonic allantois—a small nearly spherical sac about three-quarters of an inch (20 millimeters) in diameter—which drops to the ground intact. Connected to the umbilical cord, it is filled with fluid containing the excretory products of the unborn young. As the birth progresses, the urogenital opening contracts every two or three seconds in a "winking" motion just before the head appears.

The baby is born enclosed in the fetal membrane. Within 10 to 15 seconds after birth, the infant becomes active, responding to gravity, heading upward toward the pouch. The sharp claws on its well-developed front feet soon tear through the fetal membrane. These claws, capping the outer surface of each digit, are used only at birth and are soon shed. Permanent claws are grown later.

At birth, the Red kangaroo, largest of all marsupials, is barely the size of a bean and weighs only about three-quarters of a gram (.026 ounce) or approximately 1/30,000 the weight of the mother. In many ways the newborn kangaroo is still very much a fetus. Its eyes and ears are rudimentary, as is the development of its hind limbs and tail. It is entirely hairless and its skeleton is completely cartilagenous. It begins to harden immediately, though, and by the time the youngster leaves the pouch its entire skeletal system will have ossified.

But the baby must first get into the pouch. Newborn kangaroos possess well-developed nostrils and forelimbs. Their lungs are also developed enough to gulp in vital air during the long climb. Aided by these powerful "arms" and sharp claws, it laboriously climbs, with part of the umbilical cord still attached, through its mother's belly fur towards the pouch. The journey usually takes two to three minutes and is accomplished with a swimming motion of the forelimbs, its tiny body rocking back and forth like a pendulum. This journey, the kangaroo's first and most important, measures only 6 or 7 inches (15 or 20 centimeters).

Except for licking the baby and the surrounding fur, the mother can do little but watch. The licking is not so much to clear a path as it is to keep the way moist and prevent her tiny infant from drying out. The wetting by the mother's tongue may also prevent the baby from sticking to the fur. The hair in the midline between the pouch and the cloaca grows upward making the climb easier.

Having reached the pouch opening, the newborn kangaroo crawls inside and, guided by scent, begins searching for one of the four teats. Once located, it closes its tiny jaws over the end of the nipple, which then expands inside the mouth, locking the infant firmly in place.

LIFE IN THE POUCH

Once firmly attached, the tiny joey continues its development, growing in the pouch just as a placental mammal would in its mother's womb. If it is a baby Red kangaroo, it will grow 2,000 fold in the six months before it ventures out again. During this time, growth is rapid; the hind legs soon develop and the hairless infant grows its first soft fur. Kangaroos grow continuously throughout life, but at a decreasing rate as they grow older.

The mother continues each day to clean the pouch with her tongue. By this licking action, she consumes the urine and feces produced by the baby, recycling about a

Opposite: This Parma wallaby's joey has grown almost too large to fit in her pouch.

A mother Eastern grey kangaroo warms herself in the morning sun.

third of the water into milk production. Licking also seems to stimulate the infant to urinate and defecate. Very young orphaned animals often need to be stroked before they are able to eliminate properly. This phenomena has been observed in many other mammal species as well.

Although the joey is firmly attached to the nipple it can be dislodged by force or accident. Alexander Collie, the British surgeon who first published a detailed account of a kangaroo birth, also witnessed several instances of joeys re-attaching themselves to the nipple. In one example, he succeeded by gentle pressure in removing a one-and-a-quarter-inch-long (32 millimeters) baby from the teat. The teat was about an inch in length and had a bulbous tip for retention by the closed-in lips of the infant. Leaving the joey unattended in the pouch, Collie discovered two hours later that it had regrasped the teat and was again actively sucking.

The pouch life of a Red kangaroo lasts about 235 to 240 days. In other species of kangaroos and wallabies, the mother-young relationship is similar but the growth rate of the joey and the length of time it spends in the pouch varies considerably. Grey kangaroos have the longest known pouch life, usually lasting from 284 to over 300 days. Brush-tailed bettongs seem to have the shortest pouch life at 90 days. Some other examples, included in ascending order are: Tasmanian bettong: 109 days; potoroo: 150 days; Yellow-footed rock-wallaby: 195 days; Swamp wallaby: 250 to 270 days; Common wallaroo: 240 days; and Red-necked wallaby: 280 days.

BORN-AGAIN JOEYS

For clarity, the infant development of the Red kangaroo, a species that has been intensively studied in Australia, will serve as a rough model for the rest of the macropod family:

The joey first releases the nipple voluntarily when about 70 days old. Its eyes open at 130 days and it first protrudes its head from the pouch when it's about four to five months old. At age six and a half months, the joey first gets out of the pouch. At this time, the youngster can be regarded as having been "born" again. These first excursions are only for a few minutes at a time; the pouch will be home for some months yet.

As the baby grows, the composition of the milk it receives steadily becomes richer with increasing carbohydrates. There are also changes to the milk's protein makeup, including the appearance of a new protein called "late lactation protein," found only in the milk of macropods. In addition, these special milk formulas are simultaneously provided by different teats in the same pouch: a low-fat liquid for a newborn young and a high-fat, high-protein liquid for a young-at-foot.

Each day, the young kangaroo spends more and more time outside of the pouch. When it wants to re-enter, the mother cooperates by bending her body downward and spreading her forelegs. The joey approaches from the front and grasps the

A Grey kangaroo joey nurses at its mother's pouch.

pouch's rim. Tumbling in head first, it then turns a complete somersault inside, so that its head is near the entrance.

If a joey becomes temporarily lost, its mother will run around looking for it, calling loudly. Red kangaroo females make a loud clucking sound when searching for their young, while the joey separated from its mother makes a high-pitched squeak to attract her. This squeak will often bring other female kangaroos over to investigate as well. As the youngster matures, however, this "lost" call becomes deeper and more like the clucking of an adult female.

A close bond forms between an emerged joey (young-at-foot) and its mother.

JOEY'S COMING OF AGE

The end of pouch life comes suddenly. The mother simply shoves the joey away: It can nurse from a teat, but it can't climb back into the pouch again. For Red kangaroos, this happens when the youngster is about eight months old. Rock-wallabies, on the other hand, have a very short interim pouch life—that is, the time

Not yet fully weaned, this young Red-necked pademelon will stay close to its mother for several more months.

between when the joey first leaves the pouch and when it has permanently vacated it. Yellow-footed rock-wallaby young have been observed to have an interim pouch life of only seven to 10 days.

The evicted youngster stays close to its mother and continues to nurse for quite some time. A Red kangaroo may not be fully weaned until it's about a year old. During this time it will learn what plants are good to eat and what animals it should run from by watching and imitating its mother. It begins to go off alone or with other subadult kangaroos. At 18 months, the young kangaroo is almost fully grown; it will be almost another year, though, before it's ready to mate.

As Mark and I left the edge of the green meadow to head back to our camp in the last glow of evening light, a series of quick movements caught our attention. A young kangaroo, full of energy, was kicking up its heels and racing around and around across the grassy arena. In a flawless moment, we stood and watched darkness slowly blot out the scene.

Opposite: A curious young Eastern grey kangaroo assumes an endearing pose.

BOOMER'S SONG:
Individual and Mob Behavior

By midday, the air temperature had risen to 111° Fahrenheit (44° Centigrade). The scorching sun was becoming unbearable for nearly all animal life. Except for a Wedge-tailed eagle spinning a slow spiral above a rock-encrusted hill, there was nothing much to see but more rocks, some sparse grass and a few stunted trees scattered along a dry water course. This arid landscape in northwestern New South Wales had become so hot, so still, that it seemed as if the whole world was simply waiting for the coolness of evening to wash over it.

For the big male Red kangaroo, lying in the meager shade of a few overhanging bushes at the base of the hill, life had indeed become a wait. At twilight he would hop out onto the nearby plain to graze on withering grasses that had been recently greened by a passing thundershower. For now, though, he was content to lie in the shallow depression he had dug in the powdery soil for his big hips. Leaning on one elbow, from a distance, he looked very much like a man taking his ease. With apparent disinterest, he lazily watched two females, or does, also lying prostrate under a nearby shrub. Constantly monitoring this almost-silent world, his big ears rotated this way and that as he analyzed some small whisper of sound. One of the females was grooming herself.

Opposite: The open plains kangaroo becomes most active when air temperatures begin to cool at sunset.

Left: Most kangaroos rest in whatever shade they can find during the hottest part of the day.

Keeping Cool in a Hot World

First she would lick her forepaws, one and then the other, and then wipe them down over her ears and face. One paw was used to rub an itchy spot inside her right ear. Finishing her head, she then sat up and licked her body from her shoulders to the tip of her tail, pausing now and then to nibble at some particularly troublesome spot.

This action roused the other resting doe, who also sat up, opened her pouch with her forepaws and thrust her muzzle inside to lick her nursing joey. Using the unique comb formed by the fused second and third (syndactyl) toes on her hind feet, she gave herself a good head and neck scratch. Then she flopped back onto the ground to periodically scratch her flank with a forepaw. Both females were beginning to pant from the heat, a trait they share with dogs and sheep to get cool.

Further up the hill, in the rocky outcroppings, a male Common wallaroo, a smaller, more stocky species of kangaroo, also lay resting, seeking relief from the heat in a small cave that overlooks the valley. Three females had been allowed to join him and they lay almost still in a heap around him. Earlier he had vigorously defended his right to use the cave by chasing away another male that had come by to investigate. On this particular hill, there were five other smaller caves and overhanging rock ledges, all occupied by male Common wallaroos. Only this one contained any females, though.

Come evening, like the Red kangaroos, the wallaroos would also travel down the rocky hill's slope to feed. Being highly territorial, though, they will not venture more than a few hundred meters out onto the plain.

Near the top of the hill, deep inside a crevice just below the rim rock, a pair of small Yellow-footed rock-wallabies shared a cool daytime refuge. Though surface temperatures might soar, this little cubbyhole remained a nearly constant 85° Fahrenheit (29° Centigrade). These two individuals were the only rock-wallabies inhabiting this particular knoll. Westward, across a small neighboring valley, a larger and more boulder-strewn promontory supported a small colony of these lovely and uncommon animals.

The big male Red kangaroo, also known as a "boomer," was beginning to feel uncomfortable in the heat. His shady spot had moved with the sun's changing position. Rousing himself to his feet, he began licking each of his forearms. Both arms were soon wet with glistening saliva. One of the does was also licking her forearms.

"This licking behavior was long a puzzle to my colleagues and me," says Dr. Terry Dawson, a kangaroo physiologist attached to the University of New South Wales. "Then we undertook an examination of the blood supply to the forelimbs by injecting the blood vessels of a dead kangaroo with liquid latex. We found that there was a dense and intricate network of superficial blood vessels in the region that the animals usually lick. Further study revealed that during heat stress, the blood flow to the region is greatly increased." Thus, when wetted, this forearm region becomes a site of significant heat transfer due to evaporative cooling. In a number of kangaroo species licking also assists the rapid return to normal body temperature after strenuous exercise.

Furthermore, the tail contains an extensive vascular network similar to that of the forearms. In the Tammar wallaby, dry heat loss from the tail accounts for about 7 percent of its total thermal radiation. The tails of potoroos and bettongs, both a kind of rat-kangaroo, become wet at high temperatures due to dense rings of sweat glands covering their nearly naked base. In the Red kangaroo, Dr. Dawson and his associates discovered, this vascular system can be closed down at very high temperatures to help minimize heat flowing into the body. To further protect itself, under conditions of heat stress and dehydration, a kangaroo can even lower its

Wallaroos and certain rock-wallabies seek protection from the high midday temperatures of summer in rocky caves such as this.

overnight body temperature so that it starts the next day a few degrees below the normal level.

A kangaroo's fur is another means of preventing overheating. Fur is thought to reduce heat loss in a cold environment, but in the desert, fur acts as an insulation from heat gain. Some furs are also excellent solar reflectors. "The summer fur of the Red kangaroo appears to be nearly ideal in giving protection to the animal against high solar radiation," says Dr. Dawson. "In this role a combination of moderate reflectivity and a high fur density are important, especially in preventing the penetration of solar radiation deep into the fur."

A trio of overheated Grey kangaroos lick their forearms in an effort to cool themselves.

HOME ON THE HOME RANGE

As a drought intensifies, Red kangaroos will disperse, seeking new feed and watering points. Summer rains, infrequent and highly localized, are important to kangaroos because they offer fresh green grass for a short time. On the plains, it is probable that a kangaroo can see and hear a rainstorm over 20 miles (30 kilometers) away. Such distances do not inhibit the movements of Red kangaroos. Often large numbers of kangaroos will converge on a wet site giving the casual observer the impression of a kangaroo plague. In one instance, researchers reported seeing over 2,000 kangaroos in one locality. They were quick to caution, however, that this did not present a true picture of the kangaroo population.

Although Red kangaroos were once thought to be nomadic, we now know, through repeated observations of the same individuals, that they use regular home

ranges. In fact, all macropod species appear to maintain some sort of home range. Common wallaroos (also known as Euros), for instance, seem to be almost territorial in their maintenance of this area. Normally, the wallaroo establishes its home range around a water source and, unlike the Red kangaroo, will not leave for greener pastures during a drought. As water sources dry up, wallaroos hole up in caves and rock shelters in order to conserve moisture. A severe and prolonged drought will often kill many of the Common wallaroos in a region.

This is not to say that wallaroos are incapable of relatively long distance movements. A four-wheel-drive vehicle passing along a nearby track once disturbed an animal that I was watching from the top of a mesa in central Queensland. As the wallaroo bounded away, I followed it with my binoculars. When it finally paused, I noted the vegetation and rock formations near it. Later, when I measured the distance, I discovered that it had hopped nearly four and a half miles (7.5 kilometers) without stopping.

HOMING INSTINCT

When kangaroos are removed from their home ranges they demonstrate an uncanny ability to find their way back. There have only been a few studies of this phenomena, but the findings have been similar: Kangaroos (such as Red kangaroos), when captured, placed in cloth bags, transported varying distances and then released, are able to find their way home fairly quickly. The maximum return distance that I am aware of is 80 miles (128 kilometers) within one week. I'm certain their capacity far exceeds this distance because during widespread drought, marked individuals have been known to roam as far as 200 miles (over 320 kilometers) in search of new grass and water.

DAILY ACTIVITY PATTERNS

Most kangaroos can be said to be crepuscular, that is, they are most active in the very early morning and late evening around sunset. This rule is not set in stone, however; nearly all kangaroos can be active throughout the night. In general, smaller kangaroo species seem to be more nocturnal than their larger cousins. Tree-kangaroos are also very nocturnal.

These patterns are quite flexible. Sometimes, such as when a misty rain persists during the day, macropods will respond by feeding and moving out into more open areas. The only kangaroo species that is considered truly diurnal (active during the day) is the Musky rat-kangaroo found in Queensland's northern rainforests. However, in biology, exceptions are often the rule. The only wild Musky rat-kangaroo I have ever seen was observed in the darkness *before* daybreak (a crepuscular time).

DISPERSAL

The dynamics of most mammal populations demand that the young of the species disperse out of the mother's home range. Strictly defined, dispersal is the movement an animal makes from its point of origin to the place where it reproduces. Dispersal helps to colonize new territories, insures a general mixing of the gene pool and

Opposite: Kangaroo species partition themselves according to their habitat preferences. In this scene, Red kangaroos utilize the lower plain while wallaroos may be found on the rocky midslope. The upper rocks and cliffs hide two kinds of rock-wallabies.

relieves overcrowding in a given area. For these animals wandering through the countryside looking for a new place to live, it's also a dangerous time. They're young, relatively inexperienced and are often killed by predators and accidents.

Little is known about kangaroo dispersal. Male Red-necked wallabies have been observed to disperse at about two years of age, while the female young of this species tend to remain in their natal home range. It's doubtful if this observation can be generalized to include the entire macropod family. However, male-biased dispersal is a common feature in mammalian populations. Correspondingly, there is also a higher mortality rate among subadult males.

FEEDING BEHAVIOR

The larger kangaroos usually graze in a standing crouch. They will eat the vegetation in a semicircle around them, walking slowly forward as they eat. Occasionally, they will hop off to a new spot. Some of the smaller macropods including the Swamp wallaby, browse more than they graze. They prefer to nibble the leaves and young stems of shrubs and herbaceous plants.

In all species, the forepaws are very useful tools when feeding. Their curved claws are used as grappling hooks for bringing edible vegetation within reach. These hand-like paws are also quite effective for holding and manipulating long stems, pushing or pulling them out of the mouth.

Kangaroos are also great opportunists. In many Australian national parks and campgrounds, the local 'roos have become habituated to human food. I've watched them pilfer bags of bread from picnic tables, eat discarded sausages, even raid trash cans in favor of their traditional foods. Perhaps grass isn't all that tasty, even to a

The larger kangaroo species usually graze in a standing crouch.

grazing animal. At night, possums and a few of the smaller kangaroo species come in to forage for any leftover treats. On Rottnest Island, the Quokkas actually queue up in anticipation for the next tour bus arrival when slices of stale bread are handed out for the amusement of the tourists.

Like all mammals, kangaroos store excess food energy in their bodies in the form of fat. In larger macropods fat accumulates especially around the kidneys; females tend to have more fat there than do males. A big female Grey kangaroo, for instance, may have more than two pounds (1 kilogram) of fat in this area of her body. It most likely acts as an energy reserve for nursing young or in times of drought.

A kangaroo's hand-like front paws are useful for manipulating food plants, grooming and fighting.

Kangaroos will sometimes raid garbage cans in favor of their traditional foods.

DRINKING WATER

Desert-adapted kangaroos hardly ever drink water, even when it's available. For the most part, they obtain the moisture they need from the green grass and forage they eat. Red kangaroos and most Common wallaroos (Euros) drink only during severe droughts.

The Tammar wallaby is found on certain islands that contain almost no fresh water. It obtains what it needs by drinking sea water. Other species eat succulent roots, dew-covered grass and leaves or, like the Agile wallaby, dig soakage holes in the ground for water. Wild pigeons, cockatoos, emus and other smaller mammals are said to benefit from the water holes dug by kangaroos.

Drinking water is important to most species of kangaroos.

KANGAROO INTELLIGENCE

Just how smart is a kangaroo? As part of my field work, I asked that question often. Opinions varied widely; some people insisted that they were extremely cunning; others compared their brainpower to that of sheep or goats. A few of the country folks I spoke with insisted that they had all the intelligence of a fence post. In any case, the question always seemed to provoke a good argument between the regular patrons in every Australian pub I visited.

There have been very few scientific studies of kangaroo intelligence. Those that have been attempted seem inconclusive, but there have been enough results to provide some indications. For example, kangaroos can be trained to select and push levers in order to obtain food.

A German scientist is reported to have trained a Red kangaroo to differentiate between seven designs drawn on paper. Only one drawing was rewarded by food. During this same time, he trained an American opossum in the same procedure, but could only get it to discriminate between two different drawings. One hundred sixty days later, the kangaroo still remembered six of the seven drawings; after only four weeks, the opossum had forgotten its two drawings completely.

Many biologists presume macropods to be lower in brainpower than perhaps they really are. An often-cited example: Kangaroos fleeing from wild dogs will let themselves be trapped against a fence. In their panic, they seem to forget they could easily escape by simply jumping over the barrier. But porpoises, which are considered to be highly intelligent, will drown if surrounded by a purse-net, even though they could easily jump over the floating cork line to freedom. Apparently the hysteria caused by a man-made barrier does them in but it has nothing to do with intelligence.

In my experience, kangaroos are equal or slightly superior in intelligence to the North American White-tailed deer. Both seem to follow strong habitual behavioral patterns but, as many hunters will acknowledge, they are capable of surprising tricks in the right circumstances.

VISION, HEARING AND SMELL

Kangaroos have excellent eyesight, especially those living in fairly open country. With large eyes located on either side of a narrow head, they have a wide field of vision. Like most grazing and potential prey animals, they seem to be particularly good at detecting movement. From the way their eyes are arranged and focused forward, I suspect that they are also capable of at least some binocular vision, a real benefit to some species such as the rock-wallabies, that must navigate in extremely rough terrain. Kangaroos also have good night vision.

Macropods seem to possess some color perception. According to one study done in the 1960s, kangaroos can see reds and blues. Ray Williams, a mammologist who worked at the University of New South Wales Cowan Field Station, confirms this claim. He has noticed that the wallabies and kangaroos in his compounds seem very wary of people wearing bright red clothes.

A kangaroo's hearing is very keen and may be the most important sense for monitoring its environment. The two large erect ears can be rotated independently to assess sounds coming from different directions; often one will point forward while the other faces toward the rear. A grazing kangaroo will frequently stop and

The head of an Agile wallaby. Estimates of kangaroo intelligence vary widely.

raise its head to look around and listen. Even while an animal is lying down, its ears are in constant motion, scanning the surrounding area.

Smell seems to play an important role in macropod social behavior. Mutual sniffing is apparently a standard form of individual recognition. In addition, smell is a vital aid in determining the sexual condition of females; a large part of a male's courting behavior is spent sniffing a female's genitals and pouch. He will also sniff at a female's urine spot on the ground.

Diseases and Parasites

Like all mammals, kangaroos are susceptible to a variety of ills. Some of the more important bacterial and viral diseases include salmonella, tetanus (which macropods are highly susceptible to, especially in northern Australia) and macropod herpes virus. Lumpy jaw is a disease that can infect free-ranging kangaroos but most often appears in captive animals. It is characterized by jaw abscesses that cause external swelling and a gangrenous tongue, and often results in emaciation and eventual death. The most significant infecting organism to be isolated in this disease is *Fusobacterium necrophorum*. Because it often attacks injured tissues, lumpy jaw is regarded as a wound infection with specific pathological changes. Although antibiotics seem to help in curing this disease, they are not 100 percent effective.

An intestinal protozoan parasite known as *Eimeria cunnamullensis* has been found to cause coccidiosis. This disease seems specific to Eastern grey kangaroos.

Other internal parasites include a number of nematode worms, most of which live in the stomach. In fact, wild kangaroos often carry an incredible number and

Kangaroos have excellent eyesight. The reddish eye-shine is the camera light being reflected from the tapetum, a structural adaptation in the eye for nocturnal vision.

variety of nematodes. The gut mass of a Grey kangaroo may contain more than 30,000 individual worms of some 20 species.

This tremendous load of internal parasites apparently does not harm the kangaroo. Whenever I had the opportunity to accompany a professional kangaroo shooter on his rounds, I would examine the stomachs of many of the animals he had killed. In every case there were nematodes present in large numbers, yet the animals seemed in good health and often had fat reserves around the kidneys. Since the shooters are paid by carcass weight, they select only the largest and most healthy looking animals.

It seems paradoxical, but a recent hypothesis put forth by kangaroo biologists suggests that the worms may not actually be completely parasitic but form, instead, a symbiotic community within the stomach of the kangaroo. We speculated earlier that perhaps the worms benefit their hosts by secreting enzymes helpful in digesting the rough forage plants eaten by macropods. Contrary to the hypothesis, however, most zoos regularly deworm their kangaroos without apparent harmful effect.

On and embedded in their skin, kangaroos can host ticks, mites, botfly larvae, and in rainforest areas, leeches. Most of these little tormentors do no lasting harm. However, a little black fly (locally called a "sandfly") with the suggestive Latin name of *Austrosimulium pestilens* can cause a kangaroo's life to become pure hell.

Normally these little biting flies are just a nuisance. But when the water recedes after one of the big floods that periodically inundate parts of the Australian interior, the sandflies propagate in astronomical numbers.

Says Bill Bonthrone, owner of Ingaby Station in south-central Queensland, "They breed in the muddy banks and they'll be here in absolutely unreal swarms for about 10 days. During this time, they'll kill kangaroos off by the hundreds. They get into their ears and noses and around the eyes. To escape this agonizing plague, some kangaroos will be driven into hollow logs. But most of them will get into billabongs (pools of standing water). You'll see them sitting in the water with just their noses sticking out. Now and then, they'll duck their heads right under. Their heads will be just black from all the flies."

Dr. Tim Clancy, of the Queensland National Parks and Wildlife Service, has observed that a severe flood-induced sandfly plague can kill up to 90 percent of the local kangaroo population. The cause of these deaths could be due to a viral infection transmitted by the sandflies, but this has not yet been confirmed.

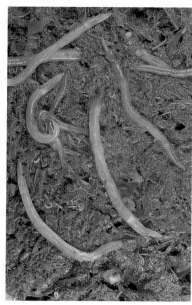

Wild kangaroos often carry a large number of nematode parasites in their gut mass. Apparently they do not harm the animals.

The Social Kangaroo

The social organization of kangaroos ranges from essentially solitary species to those living in fairly well-defined groups, called mobs. Throughout the kangaroo's evolutionary history there has been a tendency toward larger size and life on the open plains. (Even so, only a few species have become true plains dwellers; most members of the macropod family have remained nocturnal forest inhabitants.) With the move from the forest, these grassland kangaroos also became increasingly social. In open terrain, a group of kangaroos has many more eyes to spot danger.

Just how social (a biological term for "gregarious") kangaroos are is still a matter of serious debate. Male territoriality, a kind of selective antisocial behavior, was probably common among early macropods. A small rat-like forest kangaroo, known as the potoroo, still exhibits territorial behavior. There are also hints of gregariousness and dominance, both clearly social attributes, in its repertoire.

Over 30 years ago, when the systematic study of kangaroos was still in its infancy, most macropod biologists considered kangaroo mobs to be the result of essentially random groupings. But at that time it was difficult to recognize

Pages 54–55: A social group or "mob" of Eastern grey kangaroos on a small prairie in Victoria, Australia.

free-ranging individuals, and almost impossible to know anything about the spatial or group relationships of specific animals.

Later, as techniques for marking individuals improved, succeeding researchers slowly realized that these groups of feeding or resting kangaroos were much more than simple aggregations. There was a subtle cohesiveness that could only be discovered by carefully observing one kangaroo's interactions with other animals.

Dr. Clancy considers kangaroos to be only moderately social. As he points out, "Kangaroos don't show cohesion like sheep or goats." Quokkas, for example, gather together at water holes and garbage dumps, but they primarily live in solitary, overlapping home ranges. However, males and females have been said to form stable pair bonds that may last for life.

"An animal obviously pair-bonded will show a broader range of social behaviors," says Dr. Clancy, "but I still would not say they're particularly social animals."

One of the most sociable species of kangaroos is the Whiptail wallaby. Whiptails are grazers, commonly found on the grassy floors of open woodlands in eastern Queensland and northeastern New South Wales. A study done in 1974 discovered that the small groups of Whiptail wallabies observed in a given area were, in reality, subgroups of a larger mob. Not surprisingly, the study found that an individual Whiptail tends to associate with the familiar members of its own mob. (A Whiptail mob may contain up to 50 individuals, comprised of subgroups of 10 or fewer individuals.)

As part of his conclusion, the investigator in this study asserts, "I am convinced that Whiptails and the members of other social species have a gregarious tendency that goes beyond mere tolerance. That is, they are 'uncomfortable' when alone, and this unspecified need for companions of any age or sex is clearly separate from the specific attractions of sex or mother-young relationships."

Two members of a Red-necked wallaby group recognize each other by smell.

As in most mammal societies, the kangaroo's basic social unit is the female and her young. A strong bond forms within this relationship that possibly continues between mothers and their grown daughters. This attachment seems to be a significant factor in group cohesion and its perpetuation. (Young males soon leave the mob or become completely independent within the group.) Another important factor is a high degree of tolerance among males and the lack of enduring pair bonds between males and females that remain in the group. Whiptail wallabies are said to have one of the least aggressive of mammalian societies.

FIGHTING AND DOMINANCE

Aggression does occur, however. Some individuals are less tolerant than others, especially when accompanying an oestrus female. In very mild conflicts between two males, one or both of the participants may simply redirect their activities into self-grooming or grazing behavior. Called "displacement behavior," these redirected activities seem to be simply a nervous outlet for something to do that does not invite aggression.

If the disturbance is more serious, then threat displays may be employed. Grey kangaroos sometimes scratch the ground and then rub their chest in the dirt or pull up clods of grass with both forefeet. Red kangaroos and Whiptail wallabies often use another conspicuous display, called the "stiff-legged walk." One animal, usually the dominant male, walks in a slow crouch around his adversary. Instead of keeping his hind feet flat on the ground, as in normal walking, he walks supported only by the toes, keeping his rump well above his head. Sometimes the back is strongly arched and the head held stiffly upward. The entire show is performed broadside to the opponent and seems calculated to exaggerate the performer's size. This particular display is often used to supplant another male from a female that is coming into heat.

When threats don't work, then a challenge to fight is given; one male simply approaches the other and stands upright. This is the fighting position and, if ignored, may lead the challenger to hit or paw at the other male, often not making contact. If the invitation to fight is still turned down, both animals may suddenly go back to grazing or just hop away from each other.

Once a challenge is accepted, the combatants will face each other, standing erect to their maximum height by stretching up on their toes. Still, they rarely ever come to blows unless both animals are of equal size and strength.

In combat, each animal grapples with the other, using its forefeet to paw at the opponent's head, shoulders and throat. During this simultaneous pawing, both animals throw back their heads to protect their eyes from raking claws. In large species, the shoulder and chest muscles are especially well developed for just this purpose.

As the action becomes more heated, one or both animals will lean back on their powerful tails and deliver heavy kicks with both hind feet. These are usually aimed at the opponent's abdomen and they hit with a heavy "thud." (Smaller kangaroos and wallabies leap toward their antagonist more quickly with less support from the tail.) The hind claws are sharp enough to disembowel but I have never heard of it happening. Usually these straight-out kicks tend to knock the opponent off balance. The testicles are also retracted to avoid injury.

Most fights last only a minute or two and may include a pause between bouts. Serious contenders, however, may battle for 10 minutes or longer before the loser suddenly withdraws from the action and ignores further challenges. The worst injuries are a few scratches or a torn ear.

Dusk and just after sunrise are the times when most fights take place, since these are the periods when kangaroos are most active and when the largest mobs form. Subadult males often get into ritualized but very active "practice" fights. These harmless contests seem to be a way of testing one's strength and agility. They also probably set the stage for the dominance hierarchy among the males of the group: The higher the male's rank, the greater is its access to breeding females. In this way, most of the offspring will be fathered by the superior males.

RARE ATTACKS ON HUMANS

In Zumstein's Campground in Victoria's Grampians National Park, I sat perched upon a split rail fence watching a group of Eastern grey kangaroos panhandle food from a family attempting to have a picnic. One of the male kangaroos was especially aggressive and would approach the table and paw at the dishes and people's legs. Several times, someone would jump up and shoo the animal away. But within moments it would come right back again. In exasperation, lunch was cut short, the dishes packed away, the kids loaded into the car (against their will) and the family was gone, presumably to a quieter spot.

I had come here for a different purpose than to laugh at these antics, though. This campground had been the site of a recent injury attack by a kangaroo. Though they are rarely used against people, those powerfully clawed forearms and hind feet seem potentially dangerous. This was only the second time I had heard of anyone being assaulted by a wild kangaroo and I wanted to learn what had happened.

A park ranger provided me with a copy of the incident report made by the officer on duty that day. A 36-year-old man was feeding a kangaroo, when it or another animal jumped from three feet away and ". . . grabbed me around the neck and scratched my face and kicked me." The victim received a large laceration in the groin area, which required about 30 stitches to close. When the ranger asked if he had seen any signs warning not to feed the kangaroos, he said no. When I visited the site, there was a large sign warning people not to feed the kangaroos. It had been there for a long time. Although the man felt that the attack was unprovoked by a dangerous animal, there seems to be some extenuating circumstances. According to one observer, the kangaroo that he had been feeding was a female and a friend was taping it with a video camera. A male that was about 15 feet away turned around and jumped on him. What may have happened was that the male was about to mate with the female and it took the man to be a threat. In any case, the videotaped incident became sensational television news material. The offending animal was quickly destroyed.

Another "attack" occurred at Zumstein's when a man held a piece of bread above a kangaroo's head to make it reach up. "It reached up, all right," the Ranger told me, "but it accidentally raked his face in the process." Finally, in an unconfirmed report, a man playing golf in Darwin was raked on both arms by an aggressive buck kangaroo.

As powerful as they are, the big kangaroos rarely attack people. However, American circuses in the late 19th and early 20th centuries sometimes featured professional boxers matched against trained kangaroos. These well-advertised performances often attracted large crowds because the kangaroo nearly always put up a spirited defense in the ring. A changing and adverse public opinion finally put an end to these bizarre exploits.

Opposite: Two subadult male Eastern grey kangaroos engage in a mock dominance battle. In another year or so, these fights will become serious and will serve to determine which male will be able to have mating rights with the group's females.

Signs of Alarm

Kangaroos are high-strung and nervous animals. They must stay constantly alert to the possibility of predators. The noise and movement of stormy weather makes them even more excitable. Wind seems to interfere with their hearing and a sudden gust will often cause the entire troop to stand up in caution. Sometimes just the swish of a branch or even the sight of a falling leaf might cause instant panic. (Kangaroo shooters report having a great deal of trouble getting within rifle range of their prey during stormy weather.)

During particularly hard rains, all the joeys will return to their mother's pouches and the group move in among the trees, if possible. Otherwise, they just stand in the open with their backs to the wind. The animals relax a bit when the rain stops and begin to dry off by grooming themselves.

When a macropod is only mildly alarmed, it will usually hop off a short distance and then stop to resurvey the situation by sitting up to look, listen and sniff the air. If the situation still does not seem right, it will begin a slow retreat out of sight.

Most kangaroos panic easily and sudden alarm from one may cause the entire group to race away explosively in all directions. Their erratic, criss-crossing flight behavior is very much like that employed by antelopes. All the zig-zagging forms tend to confuse a predator and make it nearly impossible to concentrate on any one individual. Like other herd animals that depend upon group warning and flight for protection, social kangaroo species are highly aware of each other's actions.

Big Thumping Feet

It is a moonless night in the mulga forest of southern Queensland and silhouettes of these bushy trees can just be discerned against the starry sky. Below the canopy, it is pitch black when I switch off my electric torch. A wet dew is forming on the leaves that I brush against as I wander along a trail leading from my small camp. In places, the track runs straight and wide and here I close my eyes to slowly, very carefully, "feel" my way through the night. It takes 15 minutes to go 40 or 50 paces, my senses straining in the darkness all the while. I am not alone, for I hear

Emus will sometimes hang around groups of kangaroos, such as these Western greys. The emus feed on insects flushed by the grazing macropods, while additional eyes to help detect danger benefit the entire mob.

muffled thumping sounds all around me. "Bumpth . . . thump" and then a rustle of leaves going away from me. Every few moments the sounds are repeated in a different direction.

I quickly switch on the light when the sounds seem near but there is nothing but the dense tangle of trees to be seen. Putting the beam up to the level of my eyes and getting down on my hands and knees finally reveals the glowing eyes of a trio of fleeing kangaroos. They stop momentarily, then "thump. . . thump," they are off into the darkness beyond the reach of my light. It is nearly dawn when I return to camp, my head filled with the sounds of the Australian night.

Kangaroos are not very vocal animals and their repertoire of sounds is rather limited. Some, like Common wallaroos, hiss or cough when they're annoyed. Disturbed Rufous rat-kangaroos execute a long drawn-out growl that resembles some sort of miniature chain saw, and courting male Grey kangaroos murmur soft clucks to their sweethearts of the moment. But foot thumping is something that is nearly universal among macropods.

It is an alarm signal, usually made by a fleeing animal stamping its hind feet harder than usual on its first few hops. The exaggerated sound, similar to the alarm signal given by rabbits, seems to carry over a fair distance and will alert all kangaroos in the area. As might be expected, thumping is a very effective interspecific cue among macropods; nearly all species will react to it by at least becoming more alert. Often they, too, will run away without waiting to see the danger.

A Willie wagtail uses a Western grey kangaroo as a convenient perch to watch for flying insects chased up by the animal's grazing.

Besides man, Dingos are the most significant predator of kangaroos on the open range.

Other than serving as a warning to other kangaroos, thumping may also be a warning to a potential predator that the thumping kangaroo is aware of his presence and any further pursuit may prove futile.

BIRD-FOLK FRIENDS

Many wild animals are known to respond to the alarm call of birds. Sometimes a persistently calling bird, such as a crow, will cause a kangaroo to hop away.

Also, kangaroos (Greys in particular), are often joined by two species of small birds, the Magpie lark (*Grallina cyanoleuca*) and the Willie wagtail (*Rhipidura leucophrys*). Apparently, the larks pick ectoparasites from the kangaroo's fur, while the little wagtails use the kangaroo as a convenient perch to watch for flying insects chased up by the grazing 'roo. Several times I've seen a kangaroo literally surrounded by a half dozen or more birds intent on keeping up with it. Similar associations between birds and large herbivores occur in grassland ecosystems throughout the world.

PREDATORS OF KANGAROOS

As wary as they are, kangaroos still have a lot of predators. Before the coming of Aboriginal man to the Australian continent, the Thylacine or Tasmanian tiger (*Thylacinus cynocephalus*, named for its striped body) was probably the only important predator of kangaroos in open country. Dog-like animals, these carnivorous marsupials were said to trot determinedly after their prey until it was exhausted.

The Dingo (*Canis familiaris dingo*), a half-domesticated dog (now gone wild) that was introduced to Australia by the Aborigines or other peoples perhaps 8,000 to 10,000 years ago, was able to outcompete the Thylacine and probably caused its extinction on the mainland. Thylacines lingered on in Tasmania (where there were no Dingos) until the 1930s, when they were shot to probable extinction by white settlers and hunters.

Dingos

Besides man, Dingos are now the most significant predator of kangaroos on the open range. In regions where Dingos have been removed to permit sheep grazing, kangaroo populations can grow up to 10 times the number as in the more natural areas where the dogs still roam. Kangaroo densities, for example, are higher on the

Both predator and scavenger, a Tasmanian devil begins to devour a road-killed wallaby.

south side of the great Dingo Fence, which runs east and west through Queensland and South Australia. Originally built to stop the spread of rabbits (which failed), the fence is considered to be the longest in the world. It's now maintained to keep Dingos out of the important pastoral areas of southeastern Australia. On the north side of the fence, Dingos are still considered to be an important pest.

A researcher conducting a study at a water hole in northwestern New South Wales once recorded that 83 Red kangaroos were killed by a group of five Dingos over a seven-week period. All except three of these kangaroos were juveniles and less than half of these were actually eaten.

Sometimes the larger kangaroos (especially males) will turn and fight when being chased by dogs. If there is water nearby, the besieged 'roo may head straight for it and wade in chest deep. If a dog is unwise enough to swim out to continue the attack, the 'roo will grab it and hold it under water until it has drowned.

A large kangaroo surveys its evening domain.

"I've always thought this was just a bush tale spun by country people," Jeoff Ross, a curator at Sydney's Taronga Zoo, told me one morning while I followed him on his rounds. "But I've actually seen it. There were four dogs attacking a kangaroo and that 'roo was just swiveling around trying to keep their heads under water or push them away with his forearms. He escaped when we interceded."

Other Predators

A variety of other animals, including feral cats, foxes, monitors, pythons, eagles and Tasmanian devils prey upon macropods of suitable size. Once, while I was watching a group of Yellow-footed rock-wallabies cavort on a rocky plateau, they were attacked by a Wedge-tailed eagle (*Aquila audax*). The eagle came from behind me, up sun and knocked the nearest rock-wallaby off its feet. Quickly recovering, it dived into a fissure in the cliff face while the rest hurriedly scattered for protective shelter. The eagle made several high passes and then went on its way. Eagles have also been observed to dive and repeatedly harass female kangaroos (Reds and wallaroos) until the mothers kick their joey out of the pouch. Small and defenseless, the young kangaroo soon becomes easy prey for the eagle. One researcher recorded a case where Wedge-tailed eagles killed an adult male Common wallaroo.

Introduced from Europe, both cats and foxes are especially damaging to the smaller wallabies and rat-kangaroos and are thought to have decimated many local populations. One side effect of having Dingos in an area is that they remove the foxes and reduce the number of cats. "Although Dingos kill large kangaroos," says Dr. Clancy, "they also inadvertently protect the smaller ones that they don't prey upon."

Feral Wildlife

Pets can have a devastating impact on local wildlife. The rare Tammar wallaby is nearly extinct on the Australian mainland, although it's still common on Kangaroo Island, located off the continent's southern coast. But Kangaroo Island is also becoming heavily populated with new houses and affluent families. Along with people come the cats, some of which have been returning to the wild. (A feral animal is a domestic animal that has returned to the wild and has established a successful breeding population.) Researchers are now predicting that the Tammar wallaby population will be wiped out by the predatory cats in five years or so unless strenuous efforts are made to protect them. In this case, conservation of one species means wiping out another.

"LESSER" KANGAROOS:
A Large and Varied Family

Biologists have had difficulty constructing a stable taxonomic classification for the diverse assemblage we call the kangaroo family. At the present time, they divide the entire group into two families, the *Potoroidae*, often loosely referred to as "rat-kangaroos," and the *Macropodidae*, which contains all other kangaroos.

Of the 57 or so living kangaroo species in the world, more than half are in the "lesser" family including all of the potoroids and many of the small to mid-sized macropods (wallabies). They range in size from the little one-pound (460-gram) Musky rat-kangaroo to the Red-necked wallaby that can weigh up to 55 pounds (25 kilograms) and stand almost 3 feet (90 centimeters) tall. All of these species live primarily on the forest floor or along the margins of woodlands.

THE POTOROIDS OR RAT-KANGAROO

Rat-kangaroos are not most people's idea of a kangaroo. They're small, beady-eyed, with short round ears. At first glance, they resemble some kind of rodent. Unlike other kangaroos, who seem to be strict vegetarians, rat-kangaroos are more omnivorous in their tastes, consuming insects, worms or even the odd fledgling bird. Their hind feet are relatively shorter than most other kangaroos and there is less difference in body size and musculature between the sexes (sexual dimorphism).

All members of this group possess a prehensile tail that is used to gather nesting material. Leaves, dried grass and fern fronds are first picked up in the mouth. Then after transferring the material to the forepaws, it is placed on the ground in front of the hind feet, which kick the stuff into the curled tail. After tightening its tail, the animal moves off to its nest site carrying a small bundle behind it.

The potoroid family includes both the longest and shortest gestation periods of all kangaroos. (Bettongs have the longest at 38 days and the Long-nosed potoroo has the shortest at 21 days.) Most potoroids are mature by the age of one year, though maturity of the males in some species may take as long as two years. Rat-kangaroos generally have a high reproductive potential that may allow up to three young per year to be raised. Potoroids are also relatively long-lived for such a small mammal, with life spans of more than seven years in the wild and up to 12 years in captivity.

Opposite: Swamp wallaby.

Before the European settlement of Australia, rat-kangaroos were widely distributed throughout the southern half of the continent. Changes created by the introduction of agriculture, domestic stock, new predators (foxes and cats) and competitors (rabbits) brought rapid declines in the numbers and ranges of many species, especially those in the more arid zones. Two species are now thought to be extinct and three others are restricted to small remnants of their former range.

Musky Rat-kangaroo

If kangaroos evolved from small possum-like tree dwellers, as scientists suppose, then the Musky rat-kangaroo (*Hypsiprymnodon moschatus*) may be a living link between these long extinct ancestors and the rest of the macropod family. The hind foot of this smallest of kangaroos still retains the original movable first toe of its ancient forebearers. In all other kangaroos the first toe has become vestigial, a useless remnant of their evolutionary history.

However, all kangaroos including Musky rat-kangaroos possess specialized grooming aids, called syndactylous claws, on their hind feet. Behind-the-shoulder, on-the-flank and around-the-ear grooming is performed with these comb-like structures.

Instead of an upright hop, like other kangaroos, this 14.5-inch- (37-centimeter-) long (including tail) kangaroo runs with a bounding four-legged gallop. Its usual mode of locomotion, when relaxed, is simply a slow version of that run. They "walk" by placing their forepaws on the ground and bringing their hindfeet forward in unison. It's similar to the "crawl-walk" of other kangaroos, but unlike them, the Musky rat-kangaroo's naked, unfurred tail does not act as a support and is usually held stretched out above the ground.

An elusive and somewhat rare animal, the Musky rat-kangaroo still inhabits a few isolated patches of rainforest in northeast Queensland, particularly in the Athernon Tablelands. They seem to prefer tall closed forest areas that are in proximity to a creek or lake. (Two of the best places to encounter them are on the walking paths that encircle Lake Eacham and Lake Barrine in the Athernon Tablelands.) Although some reserve areas are set aside, much of the Musky

Musky rat-kangaroo.

Long-nosed potoroo.

rat-kangaroo's habitat is vulnerable to agricultural clearing. At present they are not considered to be endangered, however.

Generally living the solitary life, this tiny kangaroo's brown coloring blends with the dark soil and leaf litter of its forest-floor home. (They do climb on fallen branches and downed trees, too.) They also possess musk glands capable of producing a strong odor.

For a nest, the Musky rat-kangaroo creates a somewhat globular basketball-sized structure from fallen leaves. The nest, which is hidden among the vines, roots and trunks littering the forest floor, appears at first glance to be an untidy pile of leaves, but one or more small entrances lead into an internal chamber lined with dried ferns and lichens.

While other potoroids are primarily nocturnal, the Musky rat-kangaroo is said to be wholly diurnal. Their most intense activity periods are in the early morning and late afternoon when they are moving about in search of food. The rest of the day and night they sleep in their nests.

This kangaroo's stomach is a simple undivided chamber and is not capable of extensive cellulose fermentation digestion. They primarily feed upon tuberous roots and fallen rainforest fruits, along with a few seeds and invertebrate critters. The blade-like premolars of their distinctive tooth arrangement are used like shears to break open the exoskeletons of insects.

The sexes are similar in appearance and color, with males tending to be slightly larger. The female's pouch opens anteriorly, like that of a normal kangaroo, and its opening is bordered by a dense fringe of long hairs. There are four nipples inside the pouch.

There is a distinct breeding season for this species extending from February to July. Mating is preceded by several days of courtship during which the male and female stand erect, fact to face, and softly touch each other's head and neck with their forepaws. The only audible sound they are reported to make is a short cough.

Of all the kangaroo species, only Musky rat-kangaroos regularly give birth to twins. The young stay in the pouch for about 21 weeks before accompanying the mother while she is feeding. Sexual maturity is reached when they are slightly more than a year old. Some reports suggest that these kangaroos form family groups consisting of adult pairs plus young. If that is true, then this species is capable of forming strong pair bonds.

Potoroos

These small, mouse-colored, pointed-nosed rat-kangaroos range from 13 to 16 inches (34 to 41 centimeters) in length (excluding the tail) and may weigh as much as 2.2 to 4.5 pounds (1 to 2 kilograms). Their habitat preferences extend from wet gullies to dry eucalyptus forests but always include a dense ground cover of shrubs or grasses. Although they apparently can survive forest fires by going down animal burrows, the loss of sheltering ground cover is critical to their continued well-being. Survivors soon disperse from burned areas and the species remains absent until regrowth has occurred.

The female potoroo's pouch contains four nipples but, like most kangaroos, only a single youngster is born and raised at a time. The duration of pouch life, however, is only about four months. In good conditions, potoroos are able to produce as many as two or three young a year. Adults may have a reproductive life-span of more than four years in the wild.

Depending on local conditions, potoroo populations can be substantially reduced by the predations of dogs, foxes and (possibly) feral cats. Habitat loss through logging and agriculture also have significant harmful effects.

The diet of potoroos consists of roots, tubers, invertebrates and underground fungi that are obtained by energetic digging with their short forelimbs. Fungi are important items on the food list because of their abundance and a high protein and calorie content. Fungi are also a good source of water and minerals.

Certain kinds of fungi (collectively called hypogeal fungi) have been recently discovered to be very significant agents in the health and productivity of the entire forest. These fungi grow underground, connected to the roots of various woody plants, particularly trees, where they form symbiotic relationships with their hosts. Their ability to concentrate biologically important elements (such as nitrogen and phosphorous) often makes them essential in the host plant's absorption. In return, the fungi obtain energy from the roots of their hosts.

In order to reproduce, hypogeal fungi form spores in underground structures, called sporocarps. They lack an active mechanism to disperse their spores, however, and are dependent upon animals for this function. Since sporocarps are both a nutritious and reliable source of food, potoroos and other small forest mammals eagerly dig them up. One study of Long-nosed potoroos showed that fungi formed as much as 66 percent of the diet for the month of June.

When the sporocarps have been eaten and digested, the fungal spores they contained are released and remain undamaged during their passage through the digestive tract. These spores are then concentrated in the animal's feces and distributed as it moves about. When conditions are suitable, some will germinate to form new hypogeal fungi.

Prior to 1875 there were two known species of potoroos living in Australia. One, the Broad-faced potoroo (*Potorous platyops*), was collected a few times in southwestern Western Australia and then never seen alive again. In his book *The Kangaroo*, Michael Archer writes:

> Bones found on the surface of some of the Nullarbor Caves, in caves on Kangaroo Island and caves in southern mainland South Australia indicate that not long before Europeans arrived, this potoroo was much more widely spread. What caused its decline is a complete mystery but it is at least some comfort to realize that responsibility for this recent decline appears to be not ours.

The other species, the Long-nosed potoroo (*Potorous tridactylus*) was one of the first mammals to be recorded from Australia. Until recently they were thought to be rather rare, but are now known to be widely (if thinly) distributed in southeastern Australia and actually quite common in Tasmania. They used to inhabit Western Australia but no living specimens have been seen there for more than 85 years.

Long-footed potoroo.

Long-nosed potoroos are distinguished by a naked patch of skin extending up onto their long tapering snout from their button-like nose. They also have a gestation period of 38 days, which is the longest reported for any kangaroo.

Although they are considered to be a solitary species, certain individuals have a tendency to congregate in small groups. When disturbed, they quickly scatter; a frightened potoroo may cover nearly 8 feet (2.5 meters) of ground between hops.

A New Potoroo

It is rare for a new species of mammal to be discovered these days, especially if the discovery was made in a well-settled region. But in 1980, after a long period of suspicion and enquiry, biologists in the southern Australian state of Victoria announced and described a new species of kangaroo, the Long-footed potoroo (*Potorous longipes*).

John Seebeck, a biologist working for the Victoria Department of Conservation and Environment, was one of the principal investigators. The story begins in June 1967, when a large female potoroo was caught in a dog trap in the forest of eastern Gippsland.

"This specimen was quite a bit larger than any other potoroo we had seen and, frankly, we didn't know what to make of it," says Mr. Seebeck. "At that stage we didn't know very much about potoroos and having one that was rather larger than some of the others didn't mean a great deal."

About a year later he received the body of another big potoroo, which had been found dead on a highway. Curious about these "giant" individuals, Seebeck tried to locate some more specimens near the areas where the original two were found. The effort went on unsuccessfully for nearly 10 years until, in the late 1970s, two more were caught . . . alive.

"As a result of that and the detailed anatomical studies that I've been doing," Seebeck allows, "we've decided that this was truly a different species." (The Long-nosed potoroo attains a maximum weight of a little over 2.5 pounds [1 kilogram]. The Long-footed potoroo weighs in around 4.5 pounds [2 kilograms].)

Since then, several more individuals have been found. All of these come from an area no larger than 30 square miles (80 square kilometers) in far-eastern Victoria. A few years ago, fox scats containing what appeared to be Long-footed potoroo hairs were found in southeast New South Wales. This evidence suggests that these rare animals may actually have a much wider range than is presently supposed.

A recent study suggests that Long-footed potoroos have a monogamous mating system with pairs living together within the same territory. They seem to prefer high-rainfall open forest areas. All animals found to date were in areas where the rainfall exceeds 44 inches (1,100 millimeters) per year.

Their favorite food seems to be hypogeal fungi, especially one known only by its unromantic name, *Mesophellia glauca*. Its sweet odor resembles pistachio-nut oil and probably helps potoroos locate the sporocarps. Attempts are now being made to start a breeding colony of Long-footed potoroos in captivity.

Bettongs

The largest members of the rat-kangaroo family (up to 7.75 pounds [3.5 kilograms]), bettongs inhabit more arid environments than other potoroids. Habitat types may range from dry sclerophyll (eucalyptus) forests to desert sandhills, but like potoroos, a cover of dense ground vegetation is favored.

Rufous bettong.

Bettongs were once generally more widespread throughout the arid and semi-arid regions of Australia than they are today. Because of agricultural habitat changes and the introduction of foxes, they have become increasingly rare on the mainland and are being gradually restricted to a few offshore islands where foxes have not yet become a problem. One species is still common on Tasmania.

Like most rat-kangaroos, bettongs build nests out of plant material that they carry in their curled tails. Being primarily nocturnal animals, they spend most of the day sleeping in one of their several nests.

Not much is known about bettong reproductive behavior. In general, a single young is born after a short gestation period lasting about 21 or 22 days. (Normal litter size is one, though twins occasionally occur.) Pouch life for young bettongs lasts from 90 to 115 days, depending upon the species. Sexual maturity ranges from five to 12 months of age.

Captive bettongs have been observed to breed throughout the year and probably do so in the wild in order to raise as many young as possible. Like most other rat-kangaroos, bettongs are considered to be solitary in their habits, except when breeding or raising young.

In the early days of European colonization, the Brush-tailed bettong (*Bettongia penicillata*) was widespread across southern Australia. Its range and numbers have since dwindled until its continued survival is in question. Predation from feral house-cats and foxes and habitat changes due to agriculture seem to be the most likely culprits in their disappearance. For example, the last recorded occurrence of the species in the state of South Australia was on Saint Francis Island in the early 1900s. One record claimed that they "swarmed" on the island when it was first taken up for agriculture in 1859. Because they were causing problems with vegetable farming, cats were apparently introduced to wipe them out.

Brush-tailed bettong.

"Furthermore, much of their range was regularly subjected to bushfires," says Michael Archer. "Their capacity to survive those fires, coupled with a diet that consists primarily of fire-resistant foods seems to have made them bushfire-dependent. Long periods without bushfires may be having a severe effect on their survival."

Remarkably, Brush-tailed bettongs are able to live in areas where they do not have access to free water. Apparently they are able to get sufficient water from their diet of bulbs, underground fungi, seeds and insects. In spite of this ability, they are now only found in the southwestern part of the continent in a few small areas of open forest. A closely allied species, the Queensland bettong (*Bettongia tropica*) inhabits open forest on the western edge of the rainforest belt of northern Queensland.

Another related species, the Tasmanian bettong (*Bettongia gaimardi*) disappeared from the mainland more than 60 years ago. Today it survives only in the open forests of Tasmania from sea level to over 3,200 feet (1,000 meters) in altitude. At the present moment its status seems secure. "They are actually quite common here," states Greg Hocking of the Tasmanian National Parks and Wildlife Service. "They're scattered throughout the northeastern half of the state and we know of over 400 sites where they currently occur. Certain areas still have quite high population densities."

Unfortunately, there is growing evidence that regular bushfires are important factors in maintaining high numbers of Tasmanian bettongs. These fires stimulate the fruiting of mycorrhizal fungi (which are an important food for the animals) and keep the grassland and forests open. But modern forestry and farming practices have all but eliminated wildfires.

Bettongs (along with other macropods) are also considered a nuisance on Tasmanian forest plantations. Citing damage to young seedlings, forest managers kill large numbers of these animals with poisoned baits. A small but growing public outcry is being ignored and these poisonings continue. In time (perhaps quite soon), these practices will significantly and permanently damage this last important bettong population.

The home range of a Tasmanian bettong can be as large as 173 acres (70 hectares) and these animals are capable of feeding trips as long as 0.9 mile (1.5 kilometers) from their nests. Bettong nests are usually well hidden among the overhanging blades of grass-hummocks. Here, in a shallow depression, they construct a foot-ball-sized structure of grass and strips of bark. Sometimes nest materials are transported from as far away as one-third of a mile (0.5 kilometer). Besides being a secure place to lay up during inactive periods, bettong nests offer important insulation to their small inhabitants during the colder months when night temperatures often drop below the freezing point.

The Burrowing bettong (*Bettongia lesueur*) is the only kangaroo that regularly digs and inhabits burrows. This unusually social species excavates large and complex tunnel systems that can have up to 120 entrances, providing home and shelter to several, or even dozens, of individuals at the same time.

They are one of the noisiest species in the kangaroo tribe and can utter a series of loud squeals, grunts, wheezes and squeaks. Like other bettongs, they emerge in the cool of the night to feed on roots, bulbs, fungi and such. They have also been known to eat dead fish on the shoreline and to scavenge from the carcasses of sheep.

In the 19th century, Burrowing bettongs were widespread across Australia and occurred over a broad range of arid and semi-arid habitat types. They are now confined to Bernier, Dorre, Barrow and Boodie islands off the northwestern coast of the continent. The smallest island, Boodie Island, is said to support only about 50 individuals. Any disturbance in the local ecology may quickly lead to their extinction. Apparently only a small part of the island is suitable for burrows.

Another extremely rare species, the Desert rat-kangaroo (*Caloprymnus campestris*) was described from three specimens in 1843. In 1931, the species

Rufous bettong in nest.

experienced a brief population explosion in the Lake Eyre Basin of South Australia. By 1935 they had vanished and have not been recorded since that time.

Although they are considered extinct, they may still continue to survive in very meager numbers: "After all," writes Archer, "it was completely unknown for ninety years and then suddenly became abundant. This suggests that it may be a plague species which survives in some small refuge when conditions are unfavorable, but which spreads rapidly when conditions are right."

The only bettong that is still common on mainland Australia is the Rufous bettong (*Aepyprymnus rufescens*). It is the largest of the rat-kangaroos and apparently can hold its own with the predators that have proved so deadly to many of the smaller kangaroo species. When molested, Rufous bettongs produce a threatening "Churrrrrrr . . . rrrrr . . . rrrrrr" sound that reminds one of a miniature chain saw. It certainly startled me the first time I heard it.

This small kangaroo prefers to live in the grassy open forests of eastern Australia where it spends its days sleeping in a well-hidden, dome-shaped nest. These nests, usually located within large grass tussocks, provide their occupants protection from detection by predators hunting by sight in daylight. Each nest is constructed in such a way that if its inhabitant is threatened, the animal can burst out and run away at full speed.

Male Rufous bettongs are said to be very aggressive toward each other. Indeed, this aggression extends into courtship between pairs. A female that is not at oestrus, and therefore unwilling to mate, will throw herself to the ground and vigorously kick at a pursuing male with her hind feet. This act is accompanied by much growling. Approaching in a tentative fashion, the male may have to shield himself with his hind legs until he can get close enough to check by the smell of her cloaca whether or not she's ready to mate.

SOME TONGUE-TWISTING MACROPODS: QUOKKAS, PADEMELONS, DORCOPSIS AND SMALL- TO MEDIUM-SIZED WALLABIES

As mentioned earlier in this chapter, the family *Macropodidae* includes all other members of the kangaroo tribe except the rat-kangaroos. The larger members of this family are primarily grass-grazers while the smaller species tend to feed more on leaves than on grass. Neither group seems to have a diet as omnivorous as the rat-kangaroos.

In macropods, the upper incisor teeth form a crescent-shaped cutting edge at the front of the mouth. The lower incisors do not rest directly against these teeth but against a tough pad on the roof of the mouth. While grazing and nibbling, the upper and lower teeth pass each other, performing a scissor-like cutting action.

Their high-crowned molar teeth eventually become flattened with use and are replaced periodically as the animals age. By bringing new teeth into play, rather than wearing down a complete set uniformly, a very abrasive range of plant materials can be consumed. In this way, the total surface area of grinding teeth brought into action during an individual's life is significantly greater than could be contained in the jaw at any one time.

In order to digest these tough plant tissues, all macropods contain a large sacculated stomach (divided into chambers) that utilizes certain fermentation bacteria to break down the cellulose and contents of the cells. The final products of digestion (mostly fatty acids) are absorbed into the bloodstream and converted into glucose by the liver.

Opposite: A Quokka feeding on the stems of a small rush plant.

Quokkas

The little Quokka (*Setonix brachyurus*) is familiar to many tourists because it is abundantly found on Rottnest Island, a resort area near Perth in Western Australia. During the peak season, nearly every beach garbage can and campground car park is attended by a company of Quokkas who crowd around looking for handouts of bread slices. Normally this species lives in dense scrub, but on Rottnest they have grown quite tame. They can be closely approached and often fed by hand.

"Quokka" is the name given by the Aborigines to this little 7-pound (3.25-kilogram) kangaroo with a distinctively short tail, less than twice the length of the head. In the late 1600s, a Dutch sea captain, named Willem de Vlamingh, saw the Quokka on this island and mistook it for a kind of big rat. In its honor, he named the island Rottnest ("rat nest"). In those days, Quokkas were extremely abundant in the moist areas along the coast of southwestern Australia. Here, they were killed for food in great numbers by Aborigines who set fire to the bush in order to drive the fleeing animals out into the open where they could be easily speared.

A new enemy, the fox, was introduced in the 1920s. By the late 1930s, the huge Quokka colonies had vanished, leaving only remnant populations on the mainland. Only on fox-free Rottnest and Bald islands are they still considered abundant. In recent years, however, their numbers have begun to increase in the extreme southwest part of the mainland.

An important factor in the Quokka's ecology, at least on Rottnest, is their use of freshwater seeps at night and habitual shelters during the day, especially during the hot season. Conditions become so harsh during late summer that many seeps dry up and finding water becomes a problem. Some individuals are said to make nightly journeys of more than 1.25 miles (2 kilometers) to reach fresh water. Others, doing without water, suffer weight loss and anemia and as a result may die. (Sheltering in the bushes by day reduces water loss.)

Quokka society is organized into family groups, with adult males dominating females and juveniles. Males also defend individual shelter spots and form a stable linear dominance hierarchy, based on age, between themselves. Group territories,

Spectacled hare-wallaby.

which may contain from 25 to 150 adults, are less well defended and may overlap with other home ranges. Very few individuals are said to move outside their group territories.

On the mainland, Quokkas seem to be able to breed throughout the year, but on Rottnest Island the breeding season is very brief. When the weather has been mild, breeding may start in January, with births 27 days later. If the season is hot, breeding might not begin until March. Pouch life for young Quokkas is about six months long and individuals generally become sexually mature at one year.

Hare-wallabies

When the European colonists began to move into the grassy inland plains of Australia, they encountered a small kangaroo whose size and behavior reminded them of hares. During the day, these animals hide under bushes or in grass clumps and when disturbed streak away at high speed.

Hare-wallabies, as a group, tend to be browsers but grass may be included in the diet. They have an efficient water-economy and are able to extract enough moisture from their food to survive without access to free water.

Of the five known species of hare-wallabies, the Eastern hare-wallaby (*Lagorchestes leporides*) is apparently extinct, since the last recorded sighting was in 1890. It has been reported that early explorers found this little kangaroo easy to tame and it would soon learn to live about the camp, eating a diet of boiled rice, biscuits and bread.

Another species, the Central hare-wallaby (*Lagorchestes asomatus*), is known only from a single skull collected from a fresh, unsexed carcass in 1932 during a prospecting expedition in central Australia. Some scholars, however, debate whether it actually represents a new species or is just an anomalous individual.

The distribution and numbers of most hare-wallabies have been in serious decline since European settlement. Part of this deterioration may be linked to the trampling and grazing of grasslands by sheep and cattle. Sharp hooves have had a pronounced effect in most of the arid regions of the continent. Another element may be due to changes in the occurrence pattern of wildfires.

Although hare-wallabies were keenly hunted by Aborigines as food, in the long run these hunts benefited the animals. In order to clear areas for easier hunting, Aboriginal hunters habitually started a series of wildfires each winter. In his book *The Kangaroo*, Professor Archer writes of this phenomenon:

> The extinction of the desert-dwelling hare-wallabies may well be linked to the destruction of the traditional Aboriginal culture. Desert Aborigines constantly burned small patches of vegetation . . . The hare-wallabies apparently need the vegetation mosaic thus created to survive. They would use the unburned areas with old bushes for shelter, and more recently burned areas with younger bushes and freshly sprouted grass for feeding. Today huge fires periodically ravage vast areas of central Australia, creating uniform vegetation patterns. The Western hare-wallaby (*Lagorchestes hirsutus*) survives only where the Aboriginal land management practices were carried out in the recent past. The National Parks and Wildlife Service is now encouraging Aborigines to burn the bush surrounding these areas as they did in the past, to ensure the survival of this species.

The Western hare-wallaby (also known as the Rufous hare-wallaby) was once common in the deserts throughout the western half of the continent. Its habitat preference appears to be sandy areas covered with spinifex grass, where this animal has adapted to a diet containing high plant fiber. The menu includes seeds, sedges and perennial shrubs.

Bridled nail-tailed wallaby, an endangered species.

Since the decline of this species, the only known populations occur in the Tanami Desert near Alice Springs and on Bernier and Dorre islands off the west coast. These island colonies are said to fluctuate remarkably with radical increases after a wildfire burn. A captive breeding program in Alice Springs has been established to help supplement the Tanami Desert population.

The Banded hare-wallaby (*Lagostrophus fasciatus*) is a strongly gregarious animal that congregates in small groups under the low branches of bushy thickets. Like other hare-wallabies, the history of this species has an all-too-familiar ring to it. Before European settlement, the Banded hare-wallaby's range extended throughout southwestern Australia. By the early 20th century they had vanished on the mainland and have not been seen there since 1906. At present, this species is found only on two offshore islands: Bernier and Dorre islands. Efforts to reintroduce the species to Dirk Hartog Island, which lost its original population in 1920, have been unsuccessful due to the predations of domestic cats on the island.

The only hare-wallaby that remains reasonably common in Australia is the Spectacled hare-wallaby (*Lagorchestes conspicillatus*). Its wide range still includes most of the northern half of the continent, though it is declining in Western Australia where frequent burning of the Spinifex grassland is resulting in loss of necessary shelter. Offshore, they remain abundant on Barrow Island.

Spectacled hare-wallabies are so named because of the prominent reddish or orange patches encircling each eye. In the Katherine region, the Aborigines call this animal "the little one with the red eye." The species' life history is not well understood, but they seem to prefer habitats of open forest, acacia thickets and Spinifex hummock grasslands. By day, they rest in shallow "scrapes" or depressions hidden under protective shrubs. They are selective browsers and include in their diet the tips of Spinifex grass and shrubs.

Breeding can take place throughout the year but there are peaks of births in March and September. Pouch life for young lasts about 150 days and they may become sexually mature by one year of age.

Vocalizations by their species are limited to a growling warning hiss and a soft clicking sound made by courting males or mothers while communicating with their young.

Nail-tail Wallabies

These small pretty wallabies have a curious horny spur, like a small fingernail, hidden in the hair at the tip of their tails. Although African lions also possess a similar structure on their tails, the function of this arrangement is totally unknown.

Another feature that distinguishes the nail-tail wallabies is their teeth. The incisor teeth are more slender than those of other wallabies and steadily decrease in size back towards the premolars. Some zoologists believe this indicates a specialization of the diet, about which practically nothing is known, except that it includes the tough and wiry roots of grass and perhaps *Melaleuca* leaves.

As a group, very little is known about these 45-inch (115-centimeter) (including tail), 14-pound (6.5-kilogram) animals. During the day they rest in a shallow scrape under a bush and when running, hold their short arms out in an awkward angle from the body. They are extremely shy and usually solitary in habits.

Like most small kangaroos, the three species of nail-tail wallabies have not fared very well since the European settlement of Australia. The smallest species, the Crescent nail-tail wallaby (*Onychogalea lunata*) has been the worst casualty. Adapted to semi-arid woodlands and desert life, this beautifully marked animal bearing a white crescent behind its forearms was common in the central and extreme western parts of the continent. The last specimens were sighted in 1956 and a fox-ravaged carcass was found in 1964. Although presumed extinct, a small relic population may someday be discovered in some isolated refuge.

The Bridle nail-tail wallaby (*Onychogalea fraenata*) once ranged over most of eastern Australia, from central Queensland to northern Victoria. By 1937, this species was also thought to have become extinct but in 1973 a small population was discovered in the Duaringa area of eastern Queensland by a fencing contractor who recognized the animal from an illustration in a national magazine. It bears a white "bridle" line running from the center of the neck down behind the forearm on each side.

Researchers subsequently discovered that this species' last population covered a territory of about 27,700 acres (11,240 hectares). The whole area was declared a refuge and is presently managed by the Queensland National Parks and Wildlife Service.

Cattle grazing and clearing land for wheat fields are the likely reasons for their decline. (Nail-tails are too large and fast to be easy prey for foxes.) Apparently, the leaf-litter from their preferred scrubland provides them with food through hard times. Recent studies have discovered that sandalwood leaves, which fall during a drought, are used by the Bridled nail-tail wallaby as a drought supplement.

When these wallabies were common, they were a popular food item with the inland Aborigines, who often hunted them with dogs and spears. They were also caught in considerable numbers with nets stretched across their runways near patches of bush. The meat was considered by many people as some of the best the bush had to offer.

The third species of this group, the Northern nail-tail wallaby (*Onychogalea unguifera*) has pulled through the environmental changes of the last 150 years better than its cousins and still occupies most of its prehistoric range over most of Australia's "top end." The largest member of the nail-tail tribe, this species attains a weight of 17 pounds (8 kilograms). Within its range it appears to be most common near watercourses. It has been reported to dig up and eat the small underground bulbs of Onion grass. Not much else is known about its biology.

Pademelons

Pademelons are small, shy, compact macropods that inhabit wet forests having a dense understory of shrubs. Typically, these 9- to 15-pound (4- to 7-kilogram) kangaroos make tunnel-like runways through the ferns, bushes and long grass of the ground cover. The name, pademelon, is said to have come from "paddymalla," an Aboriginal term for small kangaroos of the forest. They were a favorite food item of the early European settlers.

There are four species of pademelons, all of which are fairly alike in appearance and habits. Unfortunately, their names are also so similar that a simple listing easily leads to confusion:

Red-legged pademelon.

1. The Red-*necked* pademelon (*Thylogale thetis*) inhabits the wet forests east of the Great Dividing Range in New South Wales and southern Queensland.
2. The Red-*bellied* pademelon or Tasmanian pademelon (*Thylogale billardierii*) was once found throughout southern Victoria and Tasmania. This species now only occurs on Tasmania and some of the islands in Bass Strait. However, they are considered pests in Tasmania and are regularly killed in large numbers.
3. The Red-*legged* pademelon (*Thylogale stigmatica*) is widespread throughout eastern Australia and is also found in southern New Guinea. Apparently they crossed over to New Guinea via the land bridge formed when Torres Strait (between New Guinea and the tip of Cape York Peninsula) was exposed by periodically receding seas. (At present, the water in the strait is a modest 45 feet [13 meters] deep.)
4. Finally, the Dusky pademelon (*Thylogale brunii*) is found only on the eastern two-thirds of New Guinea and some of its larger associated islands.

This last species was named in honor of the Dutch painter C. de Bruijn, who provided Europe with the first accurate description of a kangaroo in 1714. This is the first kangaroo to be given a scientific name. It had been seen on Java, in the Dutch governor's garden, where it was being kept as a pet. Apparently, it had been brought there by travelers from New Guinea.

Although pademelons have suffered a reduction in habitat because of wholesale land-clearing practices, they are still fairly common wherever their forest or at least a mosaic of forest is still intact. A radio-tracking study of Red-necked pademelons showed that they inhabit only the edges of the forest and rarely travel more than 1,600 feet (500 meters) inside and never more than 230 feet (70 meters) out onto an adjoining pasture. Apparently, the many forest/pasture edges created by "small unit" clearing are beneficial to the pademelons.

Pademelons eat a broad range of grasses, herbs and shrubs but there is a decided preference for green shoots rather than dry material. Generally, they remain in the forest during the day, foraging and basking in whatever sunlight penetrates the canopy. Only at dusk do they come out into the open to feed.

In New Guinea, this same pattern of behavior is displayed by the Dusky pademelon where the high mountain forests of the interior meet the subalpine grasslands.

Male pademelons are usually much larger than females. Not much is known about their reproductive behavior but they appear to be continuous breeders, with a marked seasonal peak, at least on Tasmania. The gestation period is around 30 days and the young may become sexually mature when one year old.

A variety of sounds are used in social behavior and may include harsh rasping hisses uttered during aggressive squabbles or soft cooing clucks from a mother to her young (or from a courting male to his female of the moment).

Dorcopsis

These are the forest wallabies of New Guinea and their generic name, dorcopsis, means "gazelle-faced." They are small, dainty kangaroos with the peculiar habit of touching only the tips of their tails on the ground when resting or sitting. The lower half of the tail lacks hairs and the tip is heavily callused.

Although the reason for this peculiar habit is not completely clear, some zoologists believe it keeps the tail out of the reach of hungry leeches. During my own observations, I've also noticed that a dorcopsis sort of "squats" above the ground in a three-point resting posture. Very little body surface is in actual contact with the forest floor.

Grey dorcopsis.

"It is notable," says Professor Archer, "that the underside of the tails of their less fortunate neighbors, the pademelons, which lack this adaptation, can become leech-infested."

Although New Guinea lies completely within the tropics, it exhibits a wide variety of life zones varying from hot, humid, swampy lowlands to high alpine grasslands. The second largest island in the world, New Guinea's most important physical feature is a series of central mountain ranges (the Central Cordillera) that dominate the interior. These mountains are one of the least biologically explored regions left on the planet. Travel here is both difficult and dangerous. Luckily, there are biologists who are willing to take on these risks.

Although it is uncertain just how many kinds of these animals actually exist in New Guinea, we presently recognize four species of *Dorcopsis* and two species of the closely related genus, *Dorcopsulus*. Fossilized remains of extinct dorcopsis wallabies found in southern Australia indicate that this group once had a much larger range.

Opposite: Red-necked pademelon.

Dorcopsis wallabies all have small rounded ears and rather large noses. The hair on the nape lies in a reverse direction in order to help shed rain when the animal is hunkered down. Lowland species such as the Brown dorcopsis (*Dorcopsis veterum*) are thinly furred, especially inside the legs; as may be expected, mountain species like the Black dorcopsis (*Dorcopsis atrata*) have denser and more luxurious fur. Only its outer hairs are black while its underfur is white. (The rest of these species are listed in the appendix at the back of this book. However, due to recent discoveries, this list is subject to revision.)

Dorcopsis wallabies are browsers that possess long premolar teeth that form a sharp pair of shears on either side of the mouth. When feeding, they pick food up with their incisors, transfer it to their hand-like forepaws, which shove it into the side of the mouth where it is bitten into pieces by the premolars.

Unlike pademelons, dorcopsis wallabies appear to stay inside the rainforest. Not much is known about their diet but the menu seems to be a varied one. One species is reported to be fond of the leaves and fruit of figs; another has been observed turning over flat stones along river banks while searching for cockroaches and other invertebrates to eat.

The social habits and reproductive biology of this group are practically unknown. But one researcher studying a captive colony of dorcopsis wallabies has recently determined that the birth of the young is followed by a postpartum oestrus and then embryonic diapause after mating (see Chapter 2).

Dorcopsis wallabies are widely hunted and trapped by New Guinean natives for food. Michael Archer and Tim Flannery mention this in *The Kangaroo*:

> Tourists who visit Koki Market in Port Moresby (Papua New Guinea) are probably familiar with the Grey dorcopsis, although they may not be aware of it. Each day a large number of smoked carcasses of this species is offered for sale, not only in Koki, but in many markets throughout southeastern Papua. Judging from the numbers caught, the Grey dorcopsis must be abundant, even in the vicinity of large towns . . .

Only about the size of a hare, the Little dorcopsis (*Dorcopsulus vanheurni*) is New Guinea's smallest kangaroo species. Tim Flannery, an Australian zoologist who conducted a mammal survey of New Guinea, reports that in certain areas large numbers of these animals are hunted and killed during droughts. The dry forest is set ablaze and the wallabies driven before the flames. In one instance almost 400 animals were captured during a single operation.

Though they are not well understood by western scientists, dorcopsis wallabies seem, for the most part, fairly secure in their numbers and distribution within New Guinea. Only extensive forest removal, such as clear-cut logging, is likely to threaten this group of macropods as a whole.

The Extinction of the Toolache Wallaby

Just one species of mid-sized macropod is thought to have become extinct since European settlement of Australia. A popular sporting target, the Toolache wallaby (*Macropus greyi*), was literally hunted to death amid widespread habitat destruction caused by the clearing of land for sheep grazing. By 1923, a small group of about 14 animals was all that remained. An attempt was made to catch them alive and move them to a protected area, but the attempt failed. No live specimens have been confirmed since 1939.

The Swamp Wallaby

As the science of taxonomy, the classification and reclassification of species, winds its convoluted way through our textbooks, animals familiar to us may suddenly be labeled with unfamiliar names. Twenty-five or 30 years ago, almost all of the smaller to medium kangaroos we call "wallabies" were grouped in a genus of their own, *Wallabia*.

Recently, however, the classification of wallabies has been revamped in an effort to incorporate new information concerning the behavior, dental structure, reproduction and genetics of the various species. For example, most wallabies have 16 chromosomes, but the male Swamp wallaby has only 11 and the female just 10. The upshot is that eight of the nine members of the *Wallabia* group were renamed *Macropus*, leaving the Swamp wallaby (*Wallabia bicolor*) the sole member of its genus.

It's doubtful if the Swamp wallaby feels lonely, though. Despite its name it is not restricted to swamps. It also inhabits moist thickets, rainforests, upland forests, open forests, heathland and dry scrublands of the dry interior. In fact, this species is one of the most widespread and common wallabies of eastern Australia. Its range encompasses a broad band of territory from Cape York Peninsula in the north to southern Victoria in the south.

The environmental changes brought about by modern culture apparently have not harmed the Swamp wallaby much. Most populations are still healthy and they seem almost ubiquitous throughout their range. In the late 1800s that range actually expanded when Swamp wallabies were introduced to Kawau Island, New Zealand. They still occur there today.

Another important factor that makes Swamp wallabies so successful is their diet. Technically they are browsers, but they can eat practically anything, including plants poisonous to humans and stock, such as hemlock and Bracken fern, without ill effects. In fact, captive Swamp wallabies have been known to devour every kind of vegetation presented to them, not to mention side courses of meat, bread, biscuits, cheese and such.

Swamp wallabies can grow as large as 60 inches (150 centimeters) long, including tail, and may weigh as much as 44 pounds (20 kilograms). Their coarse brown fur often has a lovely "grizzled" look on some parts of the body. They are also marked on each cheek with a light yellow stripe and, in some regions, the tip of the tail is colored a contrasting white. (Often, my only view of this species has been a fleeting brown form that disappeared into the evening bush. That white tail-tip was usually the best clue that the blur I had seen was a Swamp wallaby.)

Breeding may occur throughout the year, but most births happen between May and August after a gestation period of about 33 to 38 days. Like most kangaroo species, the Swamp wallaby exhibits embryonic diapause (see Chapter 2) during reproduction but the actual mating takes place up to eight days *before* the birth of the older fetus. Most other species mate after birth has occurred.

Pouch life for young Swamp wallabies lasts up to nine months and their sexual maturity may begin as early as 15 months of age.

The *Macropus* Wallabies

Just what is the difference between a "kangaroo" and a "wallaby"? Especially when they are all in the same genus, *Macropus*? This distinction, it turns out, hinges on arbitrary cutoff points and there are two rule-of-thumb measurements that can be used for making a determination. One alleges that all species of adult kangaroos are larger than 44 pounds (20 kilograms) and that all wallabies are smaller. The

A Swamp wallaby streaks for cover.

Parma wallabies.

other assumption maintains that wallabies have hind feet shorter than 10 inches. Of course, all of this is just an exercise in terminology; when it comes right down to it, both groups are really kangaroos.

Of this group, only one species, the Toolache wallaby (*Macropus greyi*), is thought to have become extinct since European settlement. No living specimens have been observed since 1927. Several other species have declining populations but most of the larger wallabies continue to reproduce successfully.

The Parma Wallaby

This fox-terrier sized macropod was first identified by naturalist and artist John Gould in 1840. Ninety years later, land clearing and the predations of introduced foxes had taken their toll; the lovely Parma wallaby (*Macropus parma*) was thought to be extinct.

Almost 30 years passed with no sign of the animal. Then a mammalogist named David Ride discovered a Parma skin that had been stored with similar looking Black-striped wallaby skins in the Australian Museum in Sydney. His search eventually led him to the tiny island of Kawau, off the coast of New Zealand, near Auckland.

A survey team, which left for Kawau shortly after the Parma skin discovery, failed to locate any living individuals, but in 1965, the team returned and discovered several hundred of these shy animals.

In the 1870s, the country estate of New Zealand's first governor, Sir George Grey, was located on Kawau. He had stocked the grounds with several species of wallabies that he had collected on his numerous expeditions to Australia. An early explorer of that continent, he became keenly interested in its wildlife. His wallabies had flourished; apparently the Parmas were even being shot as pests by the local farmers.

Following this discovery, several zoos rushed to create captive breeding colonies with the ultimate goal of reestablishing Parmas on the mainland. But soon after the Kawau discovery, several individuals were found in their original habitat in New South Wales. Since then, other mainland populations have been located. The species, though rare and rather thinly distributed, is presumed to be in no danger of extinction at the moment.

The Parma's optimum habitat appears to be wet eucalyptus forests that have an understory consisting of thick shrubby areas interspersed with patches of grass. However, some animals have been found living in drier forests.

Females may become sexually mature as early 12 months of age. Most young are born between February and June after a gestation period of about 35 days.

The Tammar Wallaby

Because they have a high reproductive rate and are easy to keep in captivity, the Tammar wallaby (*Macropus eugenii*) has been nicknamed the "lab rat" of Australian biology. Probably more has been learned about this 15- to 22-pound (7- to 10-kilogram) animal's physiology than about any other macropod except the Red kangaroo.

The Tammar was the first Australian macropod to be seen by a European. It was in 1629 and Dutch navigator Francisco Pelsaert had been shipwrecked on Houtman's Abrolhos, a group of islands off the west coast. Here, between threats of mutiny by his crew, he observed and noted this animal's existence and, after peering into a female's pouch, even made comments about its reproduction. He wrongly concluded, however, that these creatures' tiny babies were formed out of the nipples they were so firmly attached to.

Two hundred years later, in 1830, a live birth of a kangaroo was witnessed and recorded by Alexander Collie, an English surgeon aboard the ship H.M.S. *Sulpher*. Ironically, the animal he had watched was also a Tammar wallaby.

At one time, perhaps thousands of years ago, Tammar wallabies were plentiful throughout Australia. Today they exist only in widely scattered mainland colonies and on about 10 offshore islands. Currently, the largest Tammar population is found on Kangaroo Island, southwest of Adelaide.

For survival, they need an abundance of low shrubs and woody thickets for cover. In some areas on the mainland, the close-packed stems of she-oaks and other brushy trees, such as heartleaf, became known to settlers as "Tammar scrub."

This kind of environment needs a periodic facelift by wildfire—once every seven years or so—to maintain its suitability for Tammars. Burning keeps thicket plants from maturing into trees that are no longer small or dense enough to provide adequate cover. Unfortunately, the present regime of agriculture has halted most of these "cleansing" and rejuvenating fires, which were promoted by the Aborigines.   *Whiptail wallaby.*

On some of the islands where Tammars live there is little or no fresh water available for much of the year. But this doesn't seem to be a problem for the Tammar wallaby, as they can exist on sea water for long periods of time. Their kidneys are very efficient in excreting excess salt. Other sources of water include licking dew and eating succulents, which contain a great deal of salty juice.

When a Tammar is at rest, it often sits on its tail, which projects forward between its legs, in the manner assumed by many female kangaroos when they are about to give birth. The Tammar's truly remarkable reproductive feature is that after mating, the delay in embryo development can be as long as 11 months. This is the record for any mammal.

After implantation, the developing embryo will be born about 25 days later, nearly a year after conception. The youngster may remain in the pouch for eight to nine months. Females are said to become mature at about nine months old (while they are still suckling), but males do not become mature until nearly two years old. Early maturity is one way a species can maintain a high reproductive potential when it is limited to raising a single offspring at a time.

Whiptail Wallaby

Named for its long slender tail, which may be more than a meter (1 yard) in length, the strikingly marked Whiptail wallaby (*Macropus parryi*) is also known as the Pretty-faced wallaby in some regions.

They are among the largest of the wallabies, with adults standing up to a height of about 35 inches (90 centimeters). Weighing up to 57 pounds (26 kilograms), these slender and graceful animals can move extremely fast when alarmed. In some districts, countryfolk have nicknamed them "fliers." Whiptails are also one of the most social species in the kangaroo family and often live in mobs of up to 50 to 60 individuals. Each mob actually consists of several subgroups whose home ranges greatly overlap with other subgroups.

Commonly found in eastern Australia, from northern Queensland south into New South Wales, the Whiptail's preferred habitat is open eucalyptus forest having an abundance of Kangaroo grass (*Themeda australis*) in the understory, especially on ridgetops and hillsides. (They are primarily grazers instead of browsers.) Generally speaking, these macropods tend to be associated with the broken topography of hill country rather than in valleys and lowlands.

Wholesale land clearing has reduced their range in some areas. But overall, the livestock graziers' common practice of girdling or felling trees to open up the forest so it can produce more grass for cattle has inadvertently resulted in a lot more Whiptail habitat. In some localities they are extremely common and are hunted commercially on a small scale.

The Agile Wallaby

Another big wallaby, attaining a maximum weight of 60 pounds (27 kilograms), the Agile wallaby (*Macropus agilis*) is the most common kangaroo in the tropical coastal zone of northern Australia. This species is also found in the lowlands of southern New Guinea.

Agile wallabies have fared well in Australia and their range is essentially the same as it was before European settlement. Not much is known about the New Guinean race except that they appear to be abundant in certain areas.

Opposite: Agile wallabies often frequent swampy lowland forests.

Below: Agile wallaby.

Red-necked wallabies.

Their preferred habitat is the open grassy forest along rivers and streams, and they're often found hundreds of miles (kilometers) inland feeding opportunistically on grasses and leaves from low shrubs and tree saplings.

Of their acceleration and speed, John Gould wrote in his 1863 *Mammals of Australia*: "It is stated to be a most agile species, readily eluding the dogs employed in hunting it by its extreme activity in leaping among the high grass; when chased it frequently seeks shelter in the thick beds of mangroves, passing over the muddy flats in such a manner as almost to baffle pursuit."

Somewhat gregarious, Agile wallabies live in groups of up to 10 individuals. In a particularly good feeding area they may form large temporary aggregations of 100 or 200 animals. The sheer abundance of this species and its effect on crops and pastures has led to its being declared a pest in some areas.

Their color is generally sandy brown above and whitish below and both sexes have a distinct light stripe on each thigh. Their young are born throughout the year with females being able to give birth about every seven months.

In areas where crocodiles are prevalent, thirsty Agile wallabies are reported to dig seepage holes in the sandbanks adjoining rivers, rather than run the risk of getting eaten while drinking from the streams themselves.

A Few More Wallabies

The last few kangaroos in this chapter are midsized macropods attaining maximum weights of 39 to 44 pounds (18 to 20 kilograms). Ostensibly, they are considered to be primarily grazers of grass, but twigs and leaves foraged from small trees and bushes seem to make up a significant part of their diet. Though all three species are very abundant and secure in their ranges, very little is known about their biology.

The first is the Black-striped wallaby (*Macropus dorsalis*), named for the black stripe running down its back from the neck to the rump. It is a shy species, preferring to stay hidden in the dense shrub layer of the forests of eastern Australia, from Queensland to northeastern New South Wales. They are very sociable amongst themselves, though, and groups of 20 or more have been discovered resting together in day "camps."

"They seem to be the only wallaby that forms truly cohesive groups," says Dr. Tim Clancy of the Queensland National Parks and Wildlife Service. "If you startle them, they hop off in single file, rather than the scatter response common to other wallabies and kangaroos."

The Western brush or Black-gloved wallaby (*Macropus irma*), a close relative of the extinct Toolache wallaby, inhabits the southwestern corner of the Australian continent. Although its body color is generally an overall grey, its hands, feet and ear tips are a vivid contrasting black. Most individuals also have a crest of black hair on the latter half of their tail. Foxes are an important predator of this species.

Finally, the grizzled Red-necked wallaby (*Macropus rufogriseus*), is one of the most common kangaroos of southeastern Australia and perhaps the most widely distributed in the world. There is a Tasmanian form, known as the Bennett's wallaby, and successful introduced colonies in New Zealand and England.

Within its native range, partial forest clearing for stock grazing appears to have had a beneficial effect on the Red-necked wallaby's numbers. In Tasmania, they are probably more abundant now than when settlement began. This is in spite of wholesale shooting and poisoning by foresters who consider them a threat to their young trees.

A Tasmanian Red-necked wallaby, locally known as Bennett's wallaby, yawns as if ready to take a nap.

SOCIAL CLIMBERS:

Rock-wallabies and Tree-kangaroos

Τhe most specialized members of the kangaroo family, rock-wallabies and tree-kangaroos, may represent the leading edge in macropod evolution. Both are extremely agile in terrain that would confound most bipeds. As their names imply, one group has adapted to life in rocky habitats; the other to the forest canopy. Since there are considerable differences in color, size and behavior between isolated populations, especially with rock-wallabies, new species are still being discovered and described. At present, 11 species (along with several subspecies) of rock-wallabies and nine species of tree-kangaroos in the family *Macropodidae* are recognized. Because of advanced new study techniques involving blood proteins and chromosome analysis, both groups may soon be taxonomically revised with a corresponding lengthening of the species list.

Left: A Yellow-footed rock-wallaby leaping from boulder to boulder.

Opposite: Yellow-footed rock-wallabies.

ROCK-WALLABIES

Toiling up the sun-beat talus slope, I stopped to wipe the sweat streaming from my face and to consider the imposing mesa I was climbing. Above me loomed the deeply fissured rock cliffs that capped this geological monolith. Somewhere overhead, I thought I saw movement, a tiny elf-like face poking over a boulder's edge. It had disappeared so quickly that I wondered if the rippling heat waves were playing optical tricks on me. Then I saw it again . . . clearly this time . . . on a different rock precipice. Another and then another appeared until there were five small faces with erect ears staring intently down at me. Their dark eyes and pointed noses seemed so appealing that I laughed and called out a friendly greeting. Abruptly, all the little heads vanished, leaving me feeling foolish and alone.

Turning to look out over the surrounding landscape, I could barely discern the blue tarpaulin that marked my camp near a dry creek bed below. I had come here to observe and photograph the prettiest and most colorful kangaroo of them all, the Yellow-footed rock-wallaby (*Petrogale xanthopus*). Once commonly hunted for their lovely pelts, a colony of these increasingly rare 14-pound (6.5 kilogram) creatures had recently been discovered on this isolated mesa jutting up from the arid bushland. There was statewide hope among conservation organizations here in Queensland that the area would soon receive the protected status of a national park.

Searching for handholds in the broken cliff face, I laboriously hauled up my daypack, tripod and camera gear to the mountain's flattened summit. As I rested, a half dozen elfin countenances popped up here and there, stared at me and then, one by one, vanished over the cliff's edge. Their agility was astonishing; some made leaps totaling more than 16 to 20 feet (5 to 6 meters) and they landed on the smallest of places. Excellent climbers, they even ascend sloping tree trunks.

The rocky rampart home of a colony of rock-wallabies.

A Black-footed rock-wallaby peers over its rock-pile sanctuary.

The Agile Hoppers

The rock-wallaby's sure-footedness is due, in part, to some important traction-device modifications to its hind feet. Those long, projecting toenails that most kangaroos possess are shortened in this animal so that they barely extend beyond the toepads. Long toenails would scrape and slip on smooth hard surfaces. The toepads, as well as the rest of the sole, are extensively granulated to permit a secure grip on rock. Additional traction is provided by a fringe of stiff hairs surrounding the sole of each hind foot.

Their tails are long and cylindrical. Unlike the tails on most other kangaroos, they are not noticeably thickened at the base and are seldom used as props for sitting. Their primary function is for balance and they are usually carried in an upward arch over the back or, during leaps, trailed like plumes streaming out from behind. The arms of an alert or fast-moving animal are often held stiffly in front of the body.

General Range and Habitat Preferences

A surprisingly meager amount of information is available about these petite kangaroos that occur from coast to coast and range in weight from 2 to 18 pounds (1 to 8 kilograms). Although they are quite common in many localities, they are limited only to mainland Australia and a few small associated coastal islands. Rock-wallabies are believed to have originated in the western part of the continent, and apparently have never made their way offshore to New Guinea or Tasmania.

Their kind have crossed some imposing barriers, though. In many areas of their range, suitable rocky outcrops are relatively near one another, from 1¼ to 6 miles (2 to 10 kilometers) apart. But in some districts, such as the undulating landscape that I was surveying from my mesa-top, distances of 60 miles (100 kilometers) or more of unsuitable and barren ground may separate one inhabited outcrop from the next. As far as I could see with binoculars, only this stone-capped hill was host to Yellow-footed rock-wallabies. Somehow, the fossil records show, individual animals have managed to cross these perilous distances and establish new colonies. Perhaps the climate was more amenable to cross-country travel in earlier days.

Highly sociable and generally living in large colonies, rock-wallabies prefer extensive rock outcrops that have deep fissures and caves in which to escape the hottest parts of the day. Over the years, the stoney trails of some established passageways become highly polished by generations of rubbing bodies and skipping feet.

The most important feeding areas are normally located at the base of these outcroppings. The rock-wallaby's usual fare is grass, but herbs, leaves and some fruits are also eaten. As in other macropods, rock-wallabies possess a large forestomach that is adapted for microbial fermentation of cellulose.

Some species that occupy extremely arid areas seem to survive without drinking water. Apparently, they obtain all of their moisture from the vegetation they eat and are able to conserve that water by resting during the day in caves that can be as much as 40° to 50° Fahrenheit (22° to 28° Centigrade) cooler than outside temperatures. One study into animal use of rock piles discovered that the air temperatures in those deep crevasses and caves between the rocks remained constantly between 80° and 90° Fahrenheit (27° and 32° Centigrade). Outside temperatures ranged from 60° to 115° Fahrenheit (18° to 46° Centigrade). Rock-wallabies living in these areas usually emerge in the late afternoon or early evening to feed.

The Sexes and Reproduction

There are no distinct color differences between males and females of a particular rock-wallaby species but males may be up to 30 percent larger than females of the same age. Females become sexually mature somewhere between one or two years of age and can potentially breed on a continuous basis because embryonic diapause is a feature of their reproduction. In reality, though, the breeding cycle is discontinuous, influenced by such seasonal factors as temperature and rainfall.

Instead of following its mother around after leaving the pouch, like most other kangaroos, young rock-wallabies often stay behind in sheltered places. They are visited periodically by the mother in order to allow the youngster to nurse.

The Rest of the Rock-wallaby Clan

The most common species of rock-wallaby is probably the Brush-tailed rock-wallaby (*Petrogale penicillata*). Its dull brown color is ornamented only by a white cheek-stripe and a long tail with a distinct brush at its end. (In its Latin scientific name, *Petro* refers to its rocky habitat, *gale* to its marten or weasel-like pointed face; *penicillus* means "a painter's brush" and the *atus* means "provided with." Literally the name means "the weasel-face that lives among the rocks having a painter's brush tail.")

It inhabits suitable rocky areas in the eucalyptus forests of inland and subcoastal southeastern Australia. Accidentally introduced into Hawaii in 1916 when dogs tore open a cage enroute to the United States, a colony of this species is now firmly established on the island of Oahu.

Another rather common species, the Short-eared rock-wallaby (*Petrogale brachyotis*), is found along the top end of northern Australia from the Kimberly region through Arnhem Land to the Gulf of Carpentaria. There seem to be at least four distinct types of the Short-eared rock-wallaby inhabiting this range. When more extensive studies have been completed, several of these forms may prove to be distinctive species.

Opposite: Brush-tailed rock-wallaby.

Like many rock-wallabies, the Short-eared rock-wallaby utilize caves for day shelters. One rather large cave that I surveyed, Cutta Cutta Cave, was being heavily used by these animals in spite of the large numbers of tourists also visiting the cave. Although the deeper recesses of Cutta Cutta Cave can be as warm as 95° Fahrenheit (35° Centigrade), the mouth of the cave stays fairly cool in relation to outside daytime temperatures. Well-worn rock-wallaby paths led into fissures around the entrance but apparently did not penetrate beyond the twilight area.

Most of the other rock-wallaby species are either rare or on their way to becoming rare. The smallest species of rock-wallaby, the Monjon (*Petrogale burbidgei*) wasn't even discovered until 1978. Perhaps the reason for its late scientific attention is the rugged, remote and restricted confines of its favored habitat. (The Aborigines of the northwest Kimberleys, where it lives, have long been acquainted with the animal, though. There it is called "monjon" by Wunambal-speaking tribes.) Not much is known about its biology, except it appears to eat mostly leaves. Pouch young have been observed in August and October.

The Nabarlek (*Peradorcas concinna*) is another little-known rock-wallaby of northern Australia. It is prettily marked and looks, to an observer from North America, a bit like a giant chipmunk. During the dry season its average weight hovers somewhere around 2.8 pounds (1.3 kilograms) but in the wet season it jumps up to 3 pounds (1.4 kilograms). This in itself is not particularly remarkable but the Nabarlek's activity pattern also shifts from diurnal and rather bold behavior in the wet season to being very secretive and completely nocturnal during the dry season. Perhaps the threat from the White-breasted sea eagle, an important predator, is diminished during the wet season.

Nabarleks are also the only kangaroos that can produce an unlimited number of replacement molar teeth. These erupt in the back of the jaw and migrate forward as the older, worn teeth are shed. During the dry season, the Nabarlek seeks out a certain fern species (*Marsilea crenata*), which grows on the edges of ponds and swamps. This particular fern contains a large amount (up to 26 percent) of extremely abrasive silica that will quickly wear down a browsing animal's teeth. Other items in the Nabarlek's diet, such as some of the grasses, also have high silica concentrations; so possessing an unlimited supply of teeth to chew the stuff with is a definite advantage. This species appears to breed throughout the year, although most young have been observed in the wet season.

Another relatively new species is the Proserpine rock-wallaby (*Petrogale persephone*). It weighs from 11 to 18 pounds (5 to 8 kilograms) and can be over 4 feet (132 centimeters) long, including tail.

Although it lives in a rather intensively settled area it was not known to science until 1976. Many local people knew about these animals, however, and have even observed them to climb trees when threatened. Because the Proserpine rock-wallaby has been recorded from only two localities in the Proserpine district of southeastern Queensland, the species has been listed as endangered. According to Michael Archer, the reasons for its decline may be related to the apparent increase in range of the neighboring Unadorned rock-wallaby.

There are no pronounced color differences between Proserpine rock-wallaby sexes but adult males are about 60 percent heavier than females.

At least five different varieties of the Unadorned rock-wallaby (*Petrogale inornata*) are known to exist. (One of them seems to be outcompeting and replacing the rock-wallaby described above.) Most varieties occur in slightly overlapping ranges across northeastern Queensland. As its name implies, the Unadorned rock-wallaby has no distinct facial markings or stripes on its generally grey to grey-brown colored body.

The Allied rock-wallaby (*Petrogale assimilis*) and Godman's rock-wallaby (*Petrogale godmani*) are a couple of other little-known rock-wallabies occurring in northeastern Queensland. Allied rock-wallabies are only found on Magnetic and Great Palm islands and a bit of the adjacent mainland. These islands were probably connected to the Australian continent during the last Ice Age when sealevels were much lower than they are now.

Godman's rock-wallaby is considered vulnerable because, like the Proserpine rock-wallaby, its territory appears to be contracting at the expense of a northward expansion in the range of the Unadorned rock-wallaby.

More widespread, but still little known, the Black-footed rock-wallaby (*Petrogale lateralis*) has at least five distinct races throughout western and central Australia. During the past few decades their numbers have steadily declined until they are becoming generally rare. Some populations seem to be locally extinct.

This species is usually a lovely reddish-brown above with a distinct white cheek stripe and a black line running down its back. One race found in eastern Queensland, however, has purple tones, especially around the head and shoulders, with no cheek stripe.

Rothschild's rock-wallaby (*Petrogale rothschildi*), is a robust species that is still common where suitable habitat remains. Its occurrence is restricted, though, to the Hamersley Range in extreme Western Australia and to a few islands in the Dampier Archipelago just offshore. These island rock-wallabies appear to be dwarf forms of the mainland species.

In coloration, Rothschild's rock-wallaby is distinguished by the top part of its head, above the eye-line, and its ears, which are both a rich chocolate brown. This severely contrasts with its lighter colored cheeks and throat and its grey neck and shoulders. This species has no cheek or dorsal stripe.

Black-footed rock-wallabies in the Macdonnell Range of central Australia. Their protective coloration closely matches the rocky soil.

The Rock-wallaby's Uncertain Future

Rock-wallabies have fared badly since their first encounters with European settlers. The beautiful skins of such species as the Yellow-footed rock-wallaby quickly whetted the appetites of fur traders. By the 1880s and 1890s, a general pattern of slaughter was well established. In an extract from a southern Flinders Ranges newspaper, the *Area Express and Farmer's Journal*, December 1, 1882, the writer succinctly expresses the prevailing attitude toward rock-wallabies and most wildlife in general:

> The best sport we had was firing at the rock-wallaby from the seat of the buggy and watching them fall down the cliffs. Fourteen we saw fall, some were wounded, but before reaching the bottom were pretty well dead. One in particular had a soft and lucky fall and came to die at our horse's feet. We were indeed loath to leave so pretty a spot. We gazed and feasted our eyes on nature's handiwork.

In some localities rock-wallaby populations were described as "virtual plagues." Some worried property owners offered local residents, whites and Aborigines alike, bounties for rock-wallaby scalps. Since the animals often drank at stock watering points, a shooter could easily bag 40 or 50 animals in a day. By 1912, the signs of decline became evident and state governments began passing laws to forbid the killing of rock-wallabies. It was an important gesture but, unfortunately, two introduced animals—the Red fox and the feral goat—have contributed significantly to the rock-wallaby's continued decline. The Red fox is an excellent climber and can pursue rock-wallabies right into their rocky refuges. Goats, on the other hand, compete directly with rock-wallabies for food and shelter. This competition for shelter has been a critical factor in the decline of the Yellow-footed rock-wallaby. Goats have been observed to physically evict rock-wallabies from heat-sheltering caves, leaving the rock-wallabies only marginal habitat with limited cover.

The evening sky silhouettes a lone rock-wallaby.

The development of tourist facilities in some areas where rock-wallabies are found may also be having a negative effect on their populations. For example, road kills and the feeding of inappropriate foodstuffs, such as bread and candy, are believed to be at least partly responsible for the decline of free-living rock-wallabies at Jenolan Caves and in Warrumbungle National Park in New South Wales.

There is still hope for the rock-wallaby clan, though. As biological survey work has proceeded, each state has responded by creating protected sanctuaries and National Parks around these dwindling populations.

The populations themselves may even be much larger than we previously suspected. Peter McCray, a biologist with the Queensland National Parks and Wildlife Service, during a population survey of the Yellow-footed rock-wallaby, found this to be especially true.

"When I was working on the survey, I would describe this pretty animal to all the land-holders," McCray related to me. "I'd even tell them something about the places they liked to live and such, but they'd almost always say, 'No, I've never seen anything like that around here, Mate.'

"Anyway, much to their surprise, I'd hunt around and suddenly find them. I think it was just that people hadn't been back into those areas. Once we had a good look about, though, we found these rock-wallabies to be reasonably common."

After the survey was completed, the total population estimate for the Yellow-footed rock-wallaby in Queensland was raised from 5,000 or 6,000 to more than 20,000 individuals.

A Brush-tailed rock-wallaby at the entrance to a den.

TREE-KANGAROOS

Roger Martin's research camp is hidden, just off the track, in a beautiful patch of northern Queensland's Daintree rainforest approximately 28 miles (45 kilometers) south of Cooktown. Here, during daylight hours, the pace of life is very slow and seems focused mostly around rewriting field notes and assessing the progress of homemade beer brewing in jugs and bottles under a roof created by a suspended tarp. In addition to Roger's husky, bearded form, there are four other people in camp: a couple visiting from England who volunteer to do the cooking, a betel-nut chewing student from Papua New Guinea and the enigmatic Charlie Roberts, a local "bushy," who pops in now and then from seemingly nowhere.

At sunset the camp begins to come to life and the evening meal is prepared and washed down with fresh beer. Headlamps, batteries, ropes and a radio-tracking receiver, along with other assorted gear, are sorted out and checked over to make sure they are in working order. By the time we leave camp, picking our way through the dark rainforest with headlamps and electric torches, it's already past 9:00 P.M. The darkened woods are quiet except for the occasional deep-throated "wook-wook" of a nearby owl. We scan the canopy with our spotlights, looking for the reflective eyeshine of a little-known animal, the Bennett's tree-kangaroo (*Dendolagus bennettiatus*). Gazing upward, my neck becomes stiff and I stumble often over exposed tree roots.

During the past two years, aided by funds from the World Wildlife Fund, biologist Roger Martin has painstakingly located and captured most of the local tree-kangaroos in this area. Presently, he has six of them fitted with radio-collars so that their movements can be studied from the ground. "By day," he says, "they can be found, hunched over in the canopy, asleep. Their long tails, which dangle inconspicuously through the web of overhead branches, are often the only visual clue that they actually are up there."

Roger's directional radio-locater, though, can penetrate that camouflage well enough to indicate just which tree they are occupying. He waves the antenna to and fro, seeking the strongest pulse from a nearby radio-collared animal. Each collar has been tuned to transmit on its own unique frequency. Somewhere in the darkness above us, this tree-kangaroo and perhaps a companion or two is moving about feeding on leaves. We carefully search the branches with our spotlights.

The platinum glow of two shining eyes finally reveals our quarry. As we stare intently upward, a grey-furred, inquisitive face with short, round ears peers downward into the dazzling beam of our lights. "This one has no radio collar!" Roger exclaims in his quiet way.

We unpack and ready the homemade tranquilizer gun. It's hard to see through the leaves but we think we can see a bit of the animal's flank. "Thwip," the tranquilizer-filled dart is fired into the canopy 60 feet (18 meters) overhead. I keep track of the time . . . three minutes, four minutes. The animal is still looking down at us; did we miss? After four and a half minutes it loosens its grip on the branches and slumps a little, then suddenly tumbles out of the canopy, crashing through the understory and hitting the ground with a heavy "Thump!"

Except for a small scratch on its nose, where it was nicked by a thorny vine, the animal is unhurt. "Tree-kangaroos are surprisingly tough," Roger says. "When they fight, they sometimes chuck each other right out of the tops of the trees." They do take falls remarkably well; occasionally when an animal is pursued or is scared, it will simply leap from the canopy. After crashing to the ground, it quickly regains its composure and hops away.

"They're not carrying internal injuries," Roger continues, "because they're animals we've been monitoring for over a year and they're still healthy.

"Incidentally, the tree-'roo we have just captured is named Dave. He's been caught before and has lost his collar in a fight with another male."

Opposite: Dr. Roger Martin and his assistant track a radio-collared tree-kangaroo in the Daintree rainforest of northeastern Queensland.

Back in camp, Dave is weighed and measured. Roger applies a bit of ointment to his scratched nose. Using a butane-fired soldering iron, he connects a lead on a spare radio-collar in order to activate its circuitry and then securely fastens the device around the sleeping animal's neck.

After about an hour, the tranquilizer begins to wear off. Dave begins to twitch and move a little. He's placed into a burlap bag, carried back to the foot of the tree he fell out of, and laid carefully on the ground. Groggily, Dave wakes up, and then slowly ascends a tree. Dr. Roger Martin's seventh radio-collar is now on the air. "Pip . . . pip . . . pip . . . pip. . ."

An Evolutionary Oddity?

Tree-kangaroos are thought to have evolved from ground-dwelling macropods in order to take advantage of the abundant leaves in the rainforest canopy. They actually returned to the trees, for the kangaroo's earliest ancestors were arboreal possum-like creatures that probably fed on insects.

In the rainforest, almost all of the food is up in the canopy; the forest floor, by comparison, is a dark place with few edible plants. Most ground-dwelling kanga-roo species that inhabit rainforests, such as pademelons, actually find much of their food on the edge of the forest where there is plenty of light to grow grasses and succulent herbs.

The existence of an unused reservoir of food is often a catalyst for evolution. By following its food source into the treetops, the tree-kangaroo found an open niche normally occupied by monkeys in other parts of the world. If monkeys had

Tree-kangaroos are surprisingly agile, moving from tree to tree with ease.

managed to colonize Australia and New Guinea, the tree-kangaroo would have probably been driven into extinction by the competition.

According to Michael Archer, some recently described fossil bones from the Wellington Caves in New South Wales appear to be the hind limbs of a tree-kangaroo at least 50,000 years old. In life, it would have weighed as much as 100 pounds (45 kilograms) and measured 6 feet (1.8 meters) long, not including its tail.

Today's tree-kangaroos are much smaller, and range from 15 to 40 pounds (7 to 18 kilograms) in weight. Although they stand only about knee high to a man, these compact kangaroos are powerfully built. One large New Guinean species is reported to be capable of crushing a menacing dog's snout with one hand.

All nine species of tree-kangaroos are grouped into the genus *Dendrolagus* (literally, "tree-climbing hare"). Two species are found on mainland Australia, while the rest inhabit the mountainous rainforests of New Guinea and a few related islands. The ancestors of the Australian species probably migrated from New Guinea across the land bridge formed at Torres Strait when sealevels were much lower. (In 1887, a third Australian species was described from an unusual specimen killed by hunters but it apparently turned out to be a hybrid that has never been seen again.)

Adaptations for Arboreal Life

The limbs of the tree-kangaroo have been readapted for life in the canopy; both fore- and hind legs are powerfully built and of nearly equal proportions. Their short, broad hind feet have cushion-like pads and are covered with roughened "non-skid" skin, while their "hands" are equipped long sharp claws to grip trunks and branches securely.

Although they can hop on the ground like other macropods, tree-kangaroos prefer to walk along tree limbs using all four feet, like a nonhopping animal. They are surprisingly agile in trees and can travel rapidly from tree to tree by leaping as much as 30 feet (9 meters) downward to an adjoining tree.

Elizabeth Procter-Grey, a researcher who has spent considerable time watching tree-kangaroos in northern Australia, described their tree-climbing ability in an article for *Natural History* (January 1990):

> To climb, they spring two or three feet off the ground, wrap their arms around the tree trunk (usually less than a foot in diameter), and place their (hind) feet pointing up, against the trunk. Then, with a quick succession of movements—arms sliding and feet hopping up behind, the animals scale the trunk . . . . On smaller branches, the animal seems more careful and deliberate, moving just one arm or leg at a time. It sometimes uses its claws to hold twigs or small vines against the palm of its hand and can even hang in this way for a short time, supporting its weight entirely with the hands.

Tree-kangaroos usually back down, either stepping or sliding, when they descend. Their long, cylindrical tail is not prehensile and serves primarily as a balancing rod.

Just behind the shoulders, in a whorl, is a very obvious parting of the fur. This is thought to be an adaptive device to help shed water during the incessant rainfall of the wet season. When tree-kangaroos are asleep in the treetops (which is something they do most of the day), their head and forequarters are hunched over, down between their hind legs. While they are in this position, secure in the fork of a branch, most of the hair points downward from the summit of the back, forming a protective "tent."

Dr. Martin preserving samples of tree-kangaroo food materials in a plant press.

A Diet of Mostly Leaves and Sleep

"Bang!" The branch at the top of the tree shudders and droops a little. "Bang!" It falls free and then lodges in a tree fork lower down. "Rats!" Roger Martin is collecting plant samples from the forest canopy with a .22 caliber rifle.

"One of our tree-kangaroos just spent three days in this spot," he says, "and I need to know what species of trees and vines are up there in order to describe it. See how the top has been stripped of foliage?" We spend several hours in this location. When the shooting is over, the New Guinean student's excellent tree-climbing ability enables us to collect those branches that haven't fallen to the ground.

"So these animals just strip a tree before moving on?" I ask.

"They'll stay around a food source they really like," Roger explains. "There's about two or three tree species in this forest that get hit hard. Interestingly, this location wasn't being touched much last year. We had noticed earlier that there were some old scratch marks, so they must have used it before. This year, though, it's getting pounded. It looks like it's being used as an alternative to the olives."

Roger Martin has collected about 92 varieties of food plants over the past month. Tree-kangaroos appear to be primarily leaf eaters, but they will also eat fruit when it is in season. However, in the rainforest, fruit is available for such a limited time that it's probably not an important item in their diet. Leaves are available all year long, but since they have low nutrient value, tree-kangaroos are equipped with big sacculated stomachs to permit large quantities to be ingested. Like other macropods, they digest their food by bacterial fermentation.

The basal metabolic rate of tree-kangaroos is very low—about 70% of the plains-dwelling Red kangaroo. Kangaroos generally have a metabolic rate that is about two-thirds of most other mammals. Pound for pound, the tree-kangaroo operates on about 45 percent of the energy that you or I need just to stay alive. This slow metabolism is an adaptation to a diet of leaves.

After feeding, a tree-kangaroo saves energy by sleeping while it digests its meal. In fact, they may sleep as much as 60 percent of the time and, since tree-kangaroos do not appear to have any regular sleeping sites or nests, they snooze wherever they feel safe from disturbance.

Social Life and Reproduction

There is very little known about tree-kangaroo biology. They are often described as solitary animals but some recent studies are beginning to prove otherwise. The basic social unit, apparently, is the adult female and her offspring.

"The social bonding between mother Bennett's tree-kangaroos and their young is really quite strong," says Roger Martin. "The young animals seem to stay around for at least two years. We have a young radio-collared male named T.J. who's three years old. Until a couple of weeks ago he was still associating with his mother."

Adult females are also very territorial and live in a well-defined area.

"Normally, I would expect the young daughters to set up territories near the mother," continues Roger. "But there must be some female dispersal because they appear to have recolonized the whole study area in the past 50 years or so." This area had been previously logged over and hunted out.

In her study of Lumholtz's tree-kangaroos (*Dendrolagus lumholtzi*), Elizabeth Procter-Grey found that the average home range of females was about 4.5 acres (1.8 hectares). The females' ranges did not seem to overlap with each other but the single male Procter-Grey radio-collared roamed over an 11-acre (4.5-hectare) area. His home range overlapped extensively with those of several females. In addition, several uncollared males were sometimes seen well within his territorial boundaries.

Once they are mature, male tree-kangaroos seem to lead a more solitary life than do females. Consequently, they sometimes scatter over a wide area in their search for unoccupied territory. It's a perilous time, for many dangers including bigger males await the young tree-kangaroo out on his own.

"Males are totally intolerant of each other," asserts Roger. "Every time an adult male runs into another, they get into a fight—face-to-face wrestling, clawing and biting—resulting in ears being chewed off and scratches all over the body. There's a one-eared male here who weighs about 13.5 kilos (30 pounds). We had a collar on him for about three weeks last year but it's hard to keep collars on males because of all the scrapes they get into. We'll be lucky if Dave keeps his collar on for more than a month."

What we know about the male tree-kangaroo's private life is sketchy. Evidently, through fighting, they establish a social hierarchy that confers mating rights to the dominant individual. This male advertises his presence around the area by smearing a scent that is produced by glands near the anus and on his chest. The perfume is a chemical "keep out" message to potential rivals that informs them of his size and rank. It may also help the females become familiar with his occupancy.

Details of tree-kangaroo reproduction are even more sketchy. They do not appear to have a distinct breeding season because joeys at all stages of development are seen year round. But, like many larger rainforest mammals, they have a long period of maternal care with a corresponding low reproductive rate. Some biologists think that the slow development of young tree-kangaroos is a direct result of their low metabolic rate. The intervals between successive births is unknown but Roger Martin is getting good information on the growth rate of the young.

"I know how old the joey is that's with this female," Roger tells me as he points towards the forest canopy. With binoculars, and a good deal of coaching, I can just discern the animal's greyish tail hanging down through the leaves and tangled branches. "I named her baby Ruth," Roger continues. "She weighs about 3 kilos (6.6 pounds) and is almost a year old."

Trichia, the mother, is just about to come into oestrus again because she's finished lactating. According to Roger Martin's studies, Bennett's tree-kangaroos apparently have a postpartum oestrus. Once the suckling stimulus from the older young stops, the tiny embryo that has been in diapause (see chapter 2) is reactivated and is soon born.

"After the birth, there should be a lot of male activity around her," Roger predicts. "I would like to witness the mating, but chances for that are very slim."

Elizabeth Procter-Grey found in her study of Lumholtz's tree-kangaroos that the youngster permanently vacates its mother's pouch when about 350 days old. This pouch life is considerably longer than that of ground-dwelling kangaroos.

Although no longer using the pouch, she reports, the young tree-kangaroo constantly follows its mother around until it is about 575 days old (about 1.5 years). During this period the two usually curl up and sleep together.

Australian Tree-kangaroos

Both of Australia's tree-kangaroo species have extremely limited ranges: the remnant rainforests of extreme northeastern Queensland south of Cooktown. Bennett's tree-kangaroo (*Dendrolagus bennettianus*), a grayish brown-colored species that can weigh up to 33 pounds (15 kilograms), occurs in both low and highland rainforest in a region between the Daintree River and Cooktown. Its total habitat area is only about 43 miles (70 kilometers) long, from north to south, in a band that averages less than 25 miles (40 kilometers) in width. Logging operations, which are still being carried out in the south part of its range, are reducing the species' available habitat. Scaly-bark trees seem to be a key food plant.

Lumholtz's tree-kangaroo (*Dendrolagus lumholtzi*), a smaller macropod with a light-colored band across its forehead, was once common in the coastal lowland rainforests of northern Queensland. Their range has now been narrowed to the higher altitudes between Kirrama and Mount Spurgeon. Like all tree-kangaroos, they spend most daylight hours sleeping, curled up like a ball in the treetops. This species does spend quite a bit of time on the ground, however.

According to Peter Johnson of the Queensland National Parks and Wildlife Service in Townsville, Lumholtz's tree-kangaroos forage on the ground for fallen fruits and buds. After feeding, they will hop up on a favorite rock to groom themselves and rest.

This species has never been observed to drink free water in the wild. Apparently, they satisfy their water requirements through the moisture contained in their food.

Tim Flannery's New Tree-kangaroo

Opposite: A Matchie's tree-kangaroo eating leaves in the rainforest canopy.

The drawing lay on top of one of the piles of papers and bones that clutter his office in the recesses of Sydney's Australian Museum. A large map of New Guinea, one of the world's least understood places, is displayed prominently on the wall. This is where zoologist Tim Flannery heads the museum's Mammal Section, and in this sanctuary he is currently planning his next expedition to the steamy jungles of Papua New Guinea. He picks up the drawing and hands it to me.

It depicts a large black tree-kangaroo with thick bear-like fur and a bright orange streak at the base of the tail. A few years ago it was completely unknown to science. Now, like a real-life "Indiana Jones," Flannery seems obsessed with returning to the forest home of this mysterious animal.

Discoveries in science are often precipitated by accident or, in some cases, by misfortune. In 1985, Dr. Flannery was collecting information about local animals at a remote village in the Torricelli Mountains of northern Papua New Guinea. There he become ill with what he thought was a case of malaria, but a dose of drugs failed to stifle the fever. The sickness dragged on and became worse.

By the time he was carried into a local missionary clinic several hours away, he was critically ill. Even though he slipped in and out of consciousness during the long trek down the trail, Flannery noticed through the fog of his fever that one of his stretcher bearers was wearing a strange animal claw talisman around his neck. Somehow, he persuaded the man to sell it to him before he blacked out again.

The attending nurse at Fatima Mission realized that he was suffering not from malaria but from scrub typhus, a disease spread by ticks. Fortunately, the necessary drugs were on hand.

When he was well enough to return to Australia, Flannery took his unusual claw to his office and soon discovered that it was like nothing he or any other scientist had seen before. Three years went by before he could return to that village in the Torricellis to search for its origin.

To the native people, the claw was not such a mystery; older men recognized it almost immediately as belonging to the large, black creatures that lived in the treetops high on the mist-shrouded mountains above their community. When fully grown, they said, the animals were more than 6.5 feet (2 meters) long, weighed more than 88 pounds (40 kilograms) and were known locally as the "tenkile." They also said that the species was becoming exceedingly rare.

Flannery spent three weeks searching for further evidence of the animal's existence without much luck. He had packed his bags and was preparing to leave the next day when a hunter came in with a young but dead "tenkile" about 3 feet long (1 meter) that his dogs had found in the forest.

"I presumed the dogs had killed it," Flannery told me. "It looked like it had just separated from its mother."

Now he had proof that the species existed. The specimen was brought back with him to Sydney for further study.

While at home, Flannery learned that another "tenkile" joey had been captured alive and it had been brought down to the same Catholic mission that he had been carried to when he was ill. Unfortunately, the animal died before the Papua New Guinea wildlife authorities could get to it.

Tantalized by these finds, Flannery returned again, this time as the head of an expedition. The group included a documentary film crew, a member of the Papua New Guinea wildlife authority, 22 local guides and porters and tree-kangaroo expert Roger Martin.

What they found was disheartening. The animal that Flannery had just "discovered" was already nearly extinct. New Guinea's largest mammal, the "tenkile" has been formally renamed the Scott's tree-kangaroo (*Dendrolagus scottae*), after the late Winfred Scott, whose endowment is enabling a program of research and conservation of this species. Unfortunately, it still exists only above 4,000 feet (1,200 meters) on the peaks of the small Torricelli Mountain Range in West Sepik. These unconnected mountain habitats were quickly dubbed "islands in the sky" by the expedition's film crew. Any development of the area will probably topple this species into oblivion.

Recently, the top of one mountain was cleared of all trees to make way for a radio repeater station and a helicopter landing pad. The project has now been abandoned, but the damage was already done. A new road being constructed through the mountains to the coast will also bring more people and more pressure

Opposite: Goodfellow's tree-kangaroo.

A large male Matchie's tree-kangaroo.

on these sanctuaries. Dr. Flannery estimates that the actual habitat of this species now occupies less than 15 square miles (40 square kilometers) of ground.

Continued local hunting pressure may have the same effect. In an area where protein is in short supply, every large animal is a prized food source. In one village, two old men, who were probably in their 60s, told the expedition about catching "tenkile" in their younger days. Each had caught more than a hundred but the younger men catch fewer and fewer; in the past few years only one or two "tenkile" have been caught.

Other New Guinean Tree-kangaroos

The smallest and most attractively colored member of the tree-kangaroo group is the Goodfellow's tree-kangaroo (*Dendrolagus goodfellowi*). Weighing around 16.5 pounds (7.5 kilograms), it has beautiful reddish-brown fur accented by a double golden stripe down the back and a long tail mottled with gold and reddish-brown. This species inhabits the mountain oak and beech forests of eastern New Guinea between 4,000 and 9,000 feet (1,200 and 2,800 meters) in altitude. Unfortunately, the future of this lovely species is questionable because its primary habitat has been extensively modified for agriculture throughout most of New Guinea. In some areas it is already locally extinct.

The Matchie's tree-kangaroo (*Dendrolagus matchiei*) is distinguished from its close relative, the Goodfellow's tree-kangaroo, by its larger size, lack of golden back stripes and solid gold tail. Sometimes referred to as the "Huon tree-kangaroo," it is found only on the mountainous Huon Peninsula and nearby Umboi Island of northern New Guinea. Although nothing is known of its diet in the wild, Flannery reports that it will eat chickens, head first, in captivity.

Doria's tree-kangaroo (*Dendrolagus dorianus*), an inhabitant of New Guinea's central mountain range, has been found up to an altitude of 13,100 feet (3,996 meters), the highest record for any macropod. Apparently the most social species of tree-kangaroo, the animals live in groups dominated by a single male and are known to play together, even with young other than their own. Females have also been observed to gang up in order to protect themselves from the actions of aggressive males. The second largest tree-kangaroo species, a large male Doria's can weigh as much as 40 pounds (18 kilograms).

The Vogelkop tree-kangaroo (*Dendrolagus ursinus*), a black-furred macropod with a bear-like face, is Indonesia's only indigenous kangaroo species. It is found only on the Vogelkop (Bird's Head) Peninsula of the western Irian Jaya portion of New Guinea.

The last two New Guinean species include the Grizzled tree-kangaroo (*Dendrolagus inustus*), considered the least arboreally adapted tree-kangaroo, and the rare Lowland tree-kangaroo (*Dendrolagus spadix*), which is known only from six specimens.

The Future for Tree-kangaroos

Hunting pressure and habitat fragmentation are the two biggest threats to the tree-kangaroos' continued existence. Although Australian species are legally protected from all hunting except by Aboriginals, continued logging and clearing of rainforest habitats still shrink their populations into smaller and smaller areas. When habitat fragmentation becomes severe, tree-kangaroos will go to the ground in order to cross to other areas. Here they become vulnerable to any attacking dog.

Also, once these isolated stocks are unable to have contact with each other, inbreeding problems may occur. It is clear that the establishment of large well-managed forest reserves are critical to the welfare of Australia's remaining tree-kangaroos.

While much of New Guinea remains wild, this huge island is experiencing more and more hunting pressure and habitat loss from a rapidly growing human population hungry for protein and a piece of ground to call home.

History has shown that only the richer "developed" nations can afford the luxury of effective wildlife management. In the so-called "Third World," the needs of the economy almost always comes first. Papua New Guinea has set aside a few small reserves and it is hoped that each successive government that emerges from that country's confused political system will have the foresight to gazette more land as national parks and forest reserves. In addition, some sort of ranger patrols and poaching enforcement must take the place of "conservation on paper." Or better still, the villagers themselves must embrace the idea of protecting forest resources, if for nothing more than their continued use by the next generation. Unfortunately, this idea of guardianship has yet to take a serious hold in much of New Guinea.

Alarmed by worldwide environmental decline, a number of zoos are beginning captive breeding programs for many threatened animals including tree-kangaroos. At the present time, there are five species of tree-kangaroos in captivity.

"Traditionally, zoos have done a terrible job at keeping these animals," says Judy Steenburg of Seattle's Woodland Park Zoo. "According to the International Zoo Yearbook, 105 Grizzled tree-kangaroos have come into captivity since the early '50s."

Although this species seems capable of a long life (more than 20 years), most of them have already died. In order to combat this trend, Judy and her colleagues are creating a tree-kangaroo husbandry notebook aimed at improving their breeding success in captivity. This manual will be available to any zoo keeping tree-kangaroos.

In time, it is hoped that a self-sustaining population of each tree-kangaroo species can be maintained and shared by the world's zoos. Should any tree-kangaroo become extinct in the wild, these captive populations would constitute the nucleus of any re-establishment effort. At least its kind will not have vanished forever.

Grizzled tree-kangaroos.

THE GREAT KANGAROOS:
Reds, Greys and Wallaroos

In common parlance, the term "kangaroo" refers to just six species of giant macropods: the Common, Black and Antilopine wallaroos, the Eastern and Western grey kangaroos, and the Red kangaroo. These are large animals that may stand 7 feet (2.1 meters) tall when fully erect and weigh up to 200 pounds (90 kilograms).

The great kangaroos generally occupy dry, sparsely wooded grasslands, but they can also be found in richly forested or exceedingly arid habitats. In Australia, these animals fill almost the same niche that antelope, bison, deer and zebras take up in other prairie regions around the world. Primarily nocturnal, great kangaroos spend most of the day lying in the shade, interrupted by brief intervals of grazing and grooming.

Left: An Eastern grey kangaroo with a joey in her pouch hops across an early morning landscape.

Opposite: A large male Red kangaroo.

An emu and a Grey kangaroo share a pool of shade cast by a eucalyptus tree.

THE GREY KANGAROOS

When the lighted horizon began changing from crimson to bright orange, it was the signal that sunrise was very near. Shivering with cold, I crawled out of the domed tent that had been my roving home for many months and scanned the nearby prairie for signs of animal life. At first glance, several clusters of people appeared to be standing here and there, but as the light cleared, the images resolved themselves into knots of alert grey kangaroos. They seemed to be waiting for something, for all were intently studying the line of eucalyptus trees near my hidden camp.

Two emus walked obliquely out of the woods beside me and onto the plain, booming their deep "thub . . . thub . . . thub" voices. The kangaroos hardly seemed to notice. Then the fiery disk of the golden sun began rising from the land, backlighting several animals. This event must have been the cue they had been waiting for, because all of them started across the grassy expanse towards my hiding spot. Leaving their nightly feeding grounds on the plain, they were heading in dozens of hopping lines for the daytime shelter of the fringing forest. Several quietly passed nearby and soon the plain lay empty and glaringly hot.

Each sunrise, for over a week, I watched that enchanting spectacle repeat itself. Technically speaking, these were Eastern grey kangaroos (*Macropus giganteus*), one of the two species of Grey kangaroos. Though it is very similar in appearance, the Western grey kangaroo (*Macropus fuliginosus*) is considered a separate species. The main differences lie in their genetic makeup and reproductive cycles. The Western grey kangaroo's mean lengths of its oestrus cycle (35 days), gestation period (30.5 days) and pouch life (42 weeks) are shorter than the Eastern grey kangaroo's. Also, the Eastern grey exhibits embryonic diapause while the Western form does not.

The range of the Eastern grey kangaroo covers the entire eastern one-third of Australia, including parts of Tasmania. The Western grey kangaroo's range extends across the southern quarter of the country but stops before reaching the foothills of the Great Dividing Range. A darker-colored race of Western grey is found on Kangaroo Island, southwest of Adelaide. Mixed populations of both Western and Eastern grey kangaroos occur on the plains of central and western New South Wales and in western Victoria/southeast South Australia where the ranges of the two species overlap.

According to Bill Poole, a biologist with the CSIRO (Commonwealth Scientific and Industrial Research Organisation) in Canberra, captive Eastern females may produce hybrids from Western males but never the reverse. No natural hybrids have yet been found in the wild.

There is one other small difference. Western grey kangaroo populations in southwestern Australia show a marked tolerance to fluoroacetate, a toxic substance that is present in many of the legumes from southwest Australia but not in those occurring in the southeastern part of the continent. Fluoroacetate, the active ingredient of the pesticide 1080, has been widely used for control of nuisance animals in Australia and is very toxic to most macropods. It has little effect on Western grey kangaroos, however.

Most other aspects of Western and Eastern grey kangaroo biology are so similar that they need not be discussed separately.

As a naturalist who grew up in America, I view the Grey kangaroo as the White-tailed deer of Australia. Both live in similar niches in habitats ranging from semi-arid scrub to forest. Both graze in open grassy areas at night and retreat into the tree line by morning. They are both similar-sized animals and even though the 'roos hop around on two legs, they still somehow remind me of deer, especially when I see one fleeing up a steep woodland hill.

Grey kangaroos can be distinguished from all other macropods by their finely haired muzzles. Five different color phases that are often regionally distinct have been recorded. Hence, in parts of their range, their dominant color may be grey, or brown, or nearly black. Male Greys also have a strong, but not unpleasant, characteristic odor.

Grass is its favored food and on this diet, says Bill Poole, the Grey kangaroo has a lower nitrogen requirement and intake of dry matter than sheep of equivalent weight. Farmers and graziers (ranchers) in much of Australia perceive this kanga-

Relaxing in the cool shade, a male Eastern grey kangaroo waits for evening before becoming active.

roo as a direct threat to their livelihood and go to great lengths to have them eliminated as pests, even though the kangaroos eat less than one-half as much food per pound as a sheep. However, as noted in the next chapter, their true worth is slowly becoming apparent.

Breeding occurs generally throughout the year, but there is a peak of births in early summer. In the southern parts of their ranges, both species are seasonal breeders and become reproductively inactive during the winter months. Any pouch young that are lost at this time are not usually replaced until the following summer.

As a female nears oestrus, the much larger males begin making close inspections. Competition between interested males sometimes leads to spectacular fights that establish dominance and mating rights for the winner.

The male's courtship routine involves frequent gentle pawing at the female's head and clutching at the base of her tail with his forepaws. Closely following the

Because Grey kangaroos are often associated with woodlands, they are sometimes locally referred to as "foresters."

female around, he coaxes her with a series of soft clucking sounds. Her occasional sharp guttural cough seems to serve as a reminder that she's not ready to mate. Copulation, when it finally occurs, may last nearly an hour.

When giving birth, the female adopts a crouching posture, tail in the normal position, hindlegs thrust forward, toes in the air. Her weight is apparently shifted to her heels. As mentioned in chapter 2, twins have been recorded but normally a single young, weighing just over .024 ounce (800 milligrams) is produced. At birth, the youngster is only about .0033 percent of its mother's weight.

"Unlike many other macropods, female Grey kangaroos do not normally come into oestrus immediately after giving birth," reports Bill Poole. "Their oestrus cycle is considerably longer than the period required for gestation."

Females become sexually mature at 17 months. Adult females attain a maximum of weight of about 70 pounds (32 kilograms); large males have been known to tip the scales at 145 pounds (66 kilograms). In unhunted populations, Grey kangaroos may live as long as 20 years. A captive specimen is known to have lived for 24 years.

The Common wallaroo prefers a rocky, hilly habitat.

WALLAROOS

The name "wallaroo" reflects the popular notion that these macropods are about midway in size between a big wallaby and a small kangaroo. Some individual males in this group, however, can attain a physique that can rival nearly any kangaroo. Adult females tend to be considerably smaller, often less than half the size of males. Currently, three species and up to four rather indistinct subspecies are recognized.

Small caves such as this provide shelter from high midday temperatures for the Common wallaroo.

The Common wallaroo (*Macropus robustus*) is probably the most widespread large kangaroo in Australia. Its range includes all but the extreme southwest and southeast, northeast and most northern portions of the continent. Because this macropod exhibits pronounced geographic color differences, the species was once divided into as many as 10 different subspecies. Although its color varies from grey in the eastern part of its territory to red in the western regions, scientists now realize that it is essentially the same animal throughout its wide range. The reddish western color phase, however, is still commonly referred to as the "Euro."

Attaining a maximum (recorded) weight of around 110 pounds (50 kilograms), the Common wallaroo can be found in a wide variety of environments, ranging from arid grassland to coastal rainforest. It is a denizen of stony rises, rocky ridges and escarpments, especially in areas where overhanging ledges and small caves provide shelter from extreme midday temperatures.

In arid zones, the importance of these caves has only recently begun to be investigated. During summer, outside air temperatures at the University of New South Wales field station near Fowler's Gap can exceed 116° Fahrenheit (47° Centigrade). Cave interiors on the other hand, can be more than 20° or 30° Fahrenheit (11° or 16° Centigrade) cooler. Not surprisingly, competition for these places is intense and occupying males will only tolerate females or subadults in the same caves. (A researcher at Fowler's Gap reported seeing as many as 12 wallaroos come out of one small cave.)

For male wallaroos, cave occupancy is on a first-come, first-served basis; the initial male occupant normally can repel any other individual's attempt to displace it from the cave. My own examinations of several cave sites indicated that they were being used even in winter, when outside nighttime temperatures can fall below the freezing point. Those animals that are not able to get into caves usually try to shelter in the shade of whatever trees or bushes they can find.

In the cool of the evening, these wallaroos leave their shelters to graze upon the grasses and shrubs available within their limited home range. According to Michael Archer of the University of New South Wales, Common wallaroos (Euros) often arrange their territories in a cartwheel-shaped pattern that is centered on a water hole, so that the maximum number of individuals have access to water. This species can also survive in low numbers where there is no free water but there must be plenty of moisture-bearing food and deep caves available.

Under ideal conditions, population densities of Common wallaroos can be as high as 80 animals per 0.38 square mile (square kilometer). A population crash following a severe drought, though, may reduce their density to less than one individual in 10 square miles (25 square kilometers).

Young wallaroos reach sexual maturity when about a year and a half to two years old. Breeding occurs throughout the year but the number of births is reduced in times of drought and may cease altogether until conditions improve. This species has a postpartum oestrus and an embryonic diapause after mating.

The Black wallaroo (*Macropus bernardus*) has only been found in the escarpment country of Arnhem Land in Australia's extreme north. The smallest member of the wallaroo group, they attain a maximum weight of about 46 pounds (21 kilograms). Very little is known about their biology. They apparently spend the day hidden in caves and warily emerge to feed on the slopes at night. In Katherine Gorge National

A male Antilopine wallaroo.

Park, I spoke to a ranger who was intrigued by these shy animals. Unfortunately, he had seen only three of them during his entire four years there.

Another, much more common, inhabitant of Australia's "Top End" is the Antilopine wallaroo (*Macropus antilopinus*). Unlike other wallaroo species, Antilopine wallaroos are highly gregarious, occurring in groups of various sizes and composition. However, females with young-at-foot and large adult males are usually excluded from these gangs. Unlike most other kangaroos, adults tend to groom each other.

"This mutual grooming," says our friend Michael Archer, "may be used to develop social bonds between individuals."

Attaining a maximum weight of 110 pounds (50 kilograms), the Antilopine wallaroo is more slender and long-limbed than its near-relatives. It is also found in flatter, more open terrain, especially where perennial grasses are a prominent component of the monsoonal woodland understory. They can be found in rocky hill country, though, where individuals are occasionally seen sharing a water hole with other wallaroo species.

During the dry season, when temperatures soar, Antilopine wallaroos remain inactive during daytime, resting in the shade, usually near a watering place. In late afternoon they become active and move out to graze. During the wet season (or on overcast days) it may be about at any time. In some areas of northern Australia it is the most common of the large kangaroos.

Not much is known about this species' breeding habits except that the young are most frequently born in March and April. Females do not appear to have a postpartum oestrus.

THE RED KANGAROO

Attaining a maximum weight of nearly 200 pounds (90 kilograms), the Red kangaroo (*Macropus rufus*) is the world's largest macropod. Superbly adapted to arid conditions, this species is found over most of the central and western portions of Australia in open country that generally receives less than 20 inches (500 millimeters) mean annual rainfall. This species' habitat preference includes scrubland, grassy prairies and even true desert. However, it is seldom found in areas where shade from scattered shrubs or trees is entirely absent.

It is a social species, living in loose seminomadic groups called "mobs" that may contain up to several hundred kangaroos. The usual cluster size, though, ranges from two to 10 individuals.

Not all Red kangaroos are red; females are usually bluish-grey in color and in many districts are known as "blue-fliers." Occasional blue-grey males are also seen and in some localities both sexes are reddish colored. Adult Red kangaroos are distinguished from other kangaroo species by a black and white patch on the side of the muzzle and a broad, white stripe extending from the corner of the mouth to the base of each ear.

The beautiful bright pinkish-red color of large males in breeding condition is not completely due to the coloring of the hair itself. The skin in the chest and throat region exudes a powdery rose-red substance that will turn a white cloth pink when rubbed against the fur in these zones. The animals are also reported to rub this powder on their backs with their hands. Although the nature of this substance is not very well understood, it probably functions as a sexual stimulant or a pheromone indicating the animal's social status. In dried kangaroo skins, the reddish color gradually fades away.

Female Red kangaroos rarely weigh more than 66 pounds (30 kilograms), about half the average size of an adult male. Breeding may occur throughout the year but

Opposite: A large male Red kangaroo standing at full height.

is more common in the spring and summer. As with other species of macropods, there appears to be no territorial defense, but a male may fight another male that challenges his mating rights to a particular female. However, in his 1977 study of this species, Australian zoologist Alan Newsome found very little evidence of established dominance hierarchies among wild Red kangaroos, ". . . though they can supplant one another individually, either passively by moving towards an opponent or physically by shoving it aside."

At Fowler's Gap research station, Ph.D. candidate Graeme Moss has learned that the sex ratio of the local Red kangaroo population is about 65 percent female and about 35 percent male. Breeding males, however, only make up about 3 or 4 percent of the population.

The gestation period for this species is about 33 days long and the youngster's eyes open in about 130 days time. The joey leaves the pouch in about eight months and, if female, may attain sexual maturity in one and a half years to three years. (Maturity may be delayed when conditions are unfavorable.) Although wild individuals have been estimated by scientists to be up to 22 years in age, the oldest known individual of this species was a captive specimen that lived for almost 16.5 years.

The Red kangaroo is a grazing animal that prefers to consume young green grasses and herbs and its local distribution is frequently influenced by the availability of this food resource. Rain in Australia's arid regions is very spotty and localized. I have watched awesome thunderstorms rage for hours only a few miles away, yet the spot I had watched from remained dry for more than two years afterwards.

Sightings of marked individual Red kangaroos indicate that they are capable of moving 19 or 20 miles (over 30 kilometers) in search of newly greened grass following a local rainstorm. How they are able to detect the location of remote wet spots, whether by sight, smell or hearing, is still not known. During widespread

A female Red kangaroo and her nearly independent joey. Females of this species are often bluish-grey in color.

drought, these animals have been known to roam as far as 200 miles (over 320 kilometers) in search of new grass and water holes.

During good years, recent studies indicate, these big kangaroos are actually rather sedentary.

"At Fowler's Gap, the home ranges of Red kangaroos varied between only 400 and 1,000 hectares (988 to 2,470 acres)," says Dr. Tim Clancy, a one-time graduate student there. "That's not all that big when compared to the range, say, of a caribou or wildebeest."

The range and population densities of Red kangaroos have increased dramatically since the arrival of European culture and the extensive development of wells and artificial watering points. If these animals have access to water, they can survive long periods without fresh greens, subsisting instead on coarse, dried grasses and withered leaves. This species is not at risk though its numbers may fluctuate widely in parts of its range in response to severe regional droughts.

To help it survive the extreme temperatures of central Australia, the Red kangaroo is desert-adapted in a number of ways. It has a powerful kidney for concentrating its urine and conserving water, a dense capillary network on the insides of each forearm, which act as efficient heat radiators when licked, and fur that is an effective solar reflector.

"When the temperature is higher than 45° Centigrade (113° Fahrenheit), the Red kangaroo does not lie down in the shade but stands hunched, thus presenting the smallest amount of surface area for the uptake of heat from the environment," writes kangaroo physiologist Terry Dawson of the University of New South Wales. "The animal's dense fur provides an almost ideal insulation against the ambient heat. To further minimize the exposure of surface area to heat radiation, the kangaroo's long, thick tail is pulled between its legs. The tail, too, has a complex network of superficial blood vessels that are involved in heat dissipation."

The Dingo (*Canis familiaris dingo*), Australia's wild dog species, seems to be the only natural predator capable of taking this large kangaroo. In one study, carried out over a seven-week period, a group of five Dingos were observed to have killed 83 Red kangaroos within 500 feet (150 meters) of a watering hole.

Kangaroos and Drought

Even though much of central Australia is arid, the plants and animals there have been fine tuned to take advantage of the periodic rains. In a normal year, perhaps as many as two or three brief showers will wet the earth in any given spot. Taken together, this small amount of moisture is enough to sustain the annual cycle of lush growth followed by a longer period of lean dryness. Drought occurs when the rains do not fall for a season, a year, or many years, if it is a long one.

Most annual plants survive droughts by forming seeds that lie dormant in the soil. Other larger, more woody plants reduce their water loss by shedding their leaves or by living on moisture stored in huge reservoir-like roots. A few shrubs and trees send wiry taproots far down in the soil to where it is still moist. In long, unbroken droughts, even these plants will suffer as ground water retreats past the reach of thirsty roots.

Like its plants, the animals of the arid regions are also finely tuned to the rhythm of sparse rainfall. Because they are vulnerable to dehydration, each of the three types of great kangaroos has developed a complex system of adaptations and behaviors that help them survive.

Grey kangaroos are the least adapted to drought in this group. Like the other big 'roos, greys are equipped with cooling capillary networks in their forearms and tails. They also rest in the shade all day and forage mostly at night. But the grey

Pages 128–29: This aerial view shows Red kangaroos congregating in a recently "greened" area.

Severe droughts can kill large numbers of kangaroos.

Although they are very mobile, most kangaroo species prefer to stay within a general home range even during drought conditions. Some species' home ranges can be quite large.

kangaroo's preference for woodlands (a more drought-resistant environment) makes it vulnerable in marginal habitats such as plains. In some areas, more than half these animals will perish during just one year of drought.

Both the Common wallaroo and the Red kangaroo are much more weather resistant. Each has developed its own strategy for survival. Like the Grey kangaroo, the Common wallaroo prefers to remain in its restricted home range, even when food and water are scarce. The wallaroo, however, has a much greater ability to withstand dehydration. They have a more efficient water metabolism, for example, and are better at concentrating their urine. Their use of caves also minimizes water loss and they have an ability to survive on food of a lower nitrogen content.

At high ambient temperatures, both Red kangaroos and Common wallaroos lose water at a rate similar to a camel or about 2 to 4 percent of their body weight per day. Each species, however, has its own behavioral approach to drought.

When times get bad, the wallaroo prefers to stay put and go through it, while the Red kangaroo does just the opposite. It is a very mobile species and readily shifts its range in response to environmental conditions, wandering hundreds of miles seeking food and moisture.

"During drought periods, Red kangaroos also have a special mechanism to ensure that a birth will take place as soon as the drought breaks," writes Michael Archer. "The mother remains constantly pregnant and each joey develops to about two months of age in the pouch, at which stage it weakens because of the lack of nutrition due to the drought and sucks less vigorously when dying. The reduced suckling stimulates the (quiescent) embryo in the womb to recommence its development."

The first baby is already dead by the time the new one is born. The mother then goes into oestrus and mates again; the resulting new embryo soon becoming dormant. This cycle may be repeated a number of times until the drought finally

A Grey kangaroo satisfyingly scratches an itchy back.

breaks. At that time, there will be a young little joey waiting to take advantage of the good season.

However, if bad conditions persist, all three species of kangaroos will cease breeding. Large population "crashes" may soon follow. During a drought, the sex ratio of adult kangaroos may shift to about one male to five females. After the drought breaks, this high proportion of breeding females helps insure the species' quick return to normal population levels. These substantial variations in population densities is the kangaroo's normal response to intermittent availability of food and water and not necessarily an indication that the species has gotten into serious trouble. After all, the cyclic occurrence of drought is not a new phenomenon.

PEOPLE AND KANGAROOS:

A Story of Exploitation and Conservation

In the faded evening light, the two fleeing kangaroos stopped momentarily to look back. One of the Aborigines I was with, a fellow named Larry, quickly handed the rifle to Peter Jadbula, whose age and rank entitled only him the right to shoot. Old Jadbula raised the similarly ancient gun and peered down its rusty sights at one of the two forms standing near a rocky outcrop over 200 yards (182 meters) away.

"Blam!" The echoing shot startled a nearby flock of cockatoos. Both kangaroos leapt into the air but only one ran away. The other fell to the ground and lay very still.

Left: A hunted kangaroo is brought back to an Aboriginal camp for cooking.

Opposite: An Aboriginal bark painting depicting a man hunting a kangaroo by Dick Tetnjan of the Gunwinggi group in western Arnhem Land.

Two of us ran down the hill to where the kangaroo was lying. The bullet had broken one forearm and passed through the heart. Whether or not it had been simply luck, this was a very impressive shot.

A few seconds later Larry arrived, shouldered the limp and bleeding carcass, and together we triumphantly walked back to the rest of the Aboriginal group waiting on the bluff. Tonight there would be a feast in camp.

This scene has been repeated in infinite variety ever since the first people arrived in Australia some 50,000 to 70,000 (perhaps even 100,000) years ago. Kangaroos are the biggest land mammals on the continent and, until very recently, supplied the largest quantity of meat to Aboriginal hunters. The weapons used have slowly changed over time, always improving in deadliness and accuracy, but the game remains the same.

THE ABORIGINAL CONNECTION

Until recently, one of the principal duties of every man in an Aboriginal tribe was to provide meat for his family and local group. Pit traps were probably the first device to be employed in this effort. Eventually, refinements such as brush fences erected along both sides of a trail to guide the animals into the hole and sharp spikes set in the bottom to impale a falling victim were added. Over the years, new tools such as nets, spears, boomerangs and dogs were slowly added to the hunter's arsenal. Finally, with European settlement of Australia, came guns.

To increase the food productivity of their environment, the Aboriginal culture had developed a system of regularly burning small patches of landscape at certain times of the year. This burning practice has been called "firestick farming" because fire in the right amount and intensity stimulates the growth of grasses, bushes and tender plants that are the principal food of kangaroos and other game. These burnings also insured that devastating wildfires did not ravage the landscape. Modern wildlife managers worldwide are now just beginning to realize that this ancient practice, technically labeled "mosaic land burning," is one of the most beneficial habitat enhancement and wildlife conservation tools at their disposal. The resulting patchwork pattern of trees, scrub and grass provides animals with both feed and unburned protective cover.

"From stories old Jadbula has told me, their burning was also used as a hunting method," says son-in-law Nigel Hunter. "Young boys weren't allowed to take part in the kills . . . they were the ones who had to go around lighting the fires. They would come in from two different directions about two kilometers (1.25 miles) apart, lighting fires as they walked. About 50 men would wait in the center and move towards where the fires were coming. As the kangaroos came fleeing through, they would get them with their spears." Unfortunately, the fires have stopped burning for many years in most of Australia and large areas are reverting into unusable scrub.

Kangaroos provided the Aborigines with other products in addition to meat. The long sinews from the tail become excellent bindings for spears and stone implements. The fur can be twisted into twine and the teeth fashioned into attractive necklaces. In the southern part of the continent, where winter temperatures may go below freezing, kangaroo skins provided people with warm furry cloaks. On the dry plains, specially prepared skins were sewn and sealed to make water bags.

Because of its significant economic value, kangaroos became a subject of great importance in Aboriginal culture. They were classified according to color, size, sex and habitat and one particular variety was often adopted as a tribal totem.

The kangaroo is also one of the most widely distributed and striking Aboriginal art motifs of Australia. Often painted on cave walls or on the underside of

Larry Atkinson singes the fur off a kangaroo before cooking it.

overhanging rocks, the Aborigines graphically depict animals in sitting or leaping postures. Sometimes kangaroos are shown pursued by a hunter or being struck by a spear or club. At one remarkable location in the Sydney-Hawkesbury district of New South Wales, there exists superb rock outline engravings of kangaroos over 24 feet long. Bark paintings from Arnhem Land in northern Australia are another example of artistic sophistication. Known as the "x-ray" style, these striking representations even include the internal organs of the animals they depict.

Cave paintings are created in areas that have special significance to the local Aboriginal clan. These spots may have religious, historical or even geographical importance to the people. Even though some of these paintings are hundreds of years old, many are updated every year as part of the responsibility that the "owners" of this land have inherited. It is said that when the last "Jungei" or caretaker family from a particular "country" has died out, then the paintings in that area are no longer updated. They may remain, though, as historic monuments for thousands of years.

Peter Jadbula is the "Jungei" custodian for an area of about 3,900 square miles (10,000 square kilometers) in Australia's Northern Territory. He is the "official" voice of that country to his people, the Jawoyns, and to the Australian government. He is also the present master of the "Dreamtime" song, the oral tradition of myth and law for his group.

"In the beginning, during Dreamtime," he says, "the kangaroo and all of the animals contributed to form the country as we know it. . . . Every animal, every tree, every plant is my relative. . . ." As I listened to his stories, I began to realize that in spite of the great high-speed technological societies that now dominate the world, Aboriginal culture has remained remarkably intact and unchanging.

KANGAROO NATIVE STYLE

The majority of Australia's Aboriginal people who live outside of urban areas still consume wild foods as part of their diet. "Bush tucker," as they call it, can be anything from yams dug from the ground and fruits from different trees to lizards, snakes, grubs, crocodiles, turtles, fish and kangaroos.

Aboriginal culture is also filled with the rigid rules of tradition, honed and perfected for thousands of years. Even when it comes to cooking food, there's a prescribed way, a law born out of respect for the particular animal that harkens all the way back to Dreamtime.

Once we had arrived back at camp, our dead kangaroo was laid down on the ground and its internal organs removed. "You've eaten guts and liver from kangaroo before?" one of my companions asked me. I shook my head. "It's really nice," he said.

A rectangular hole about 4 feet long and 2 feet wide (1.2 meters by .6 meter) had been dug into the ground to serve as a pit oven. A pile of firewood was stacked inside and lit with a disposable butane cigarette lighter.

"The next thing you do is break the kangaroo's legs by dislocating them," Nigel told me. "Then we tie the feet up in a very prescribed manner with bush string and throw the carcass on the fire in order to burn the hair off."

After removing the thoroughly singed kangaroo, the men then placed a number of rocks on top of the fire in order to heat them. When the rocks and walls of the pit were very hot, the fire was allowed to die into glowing coals. A few of the hot rocks were placed inside the kangaroo in strategic places to assist in cooking it and a bundle of wet leaves was stuffed inside the chest cavity to help moisten the meat. Then the carcass was placed on top of the bed of coals and covered with a mixture of hot rocks and coals. The top of the oven was covered with a sheet of corrugated roofing tin and sealed with a 4-inch (10-centimeter) coating of dirt.

"In the olden days we used the bark from the Paperbark tree to cover the pit," Nigel explained. "Now that the oven is sealed, all we have to do is go over and sit by the campfire until the kangaroo is ready."

"How do you know when it's done?" I asked.

"We just know," Nigel asserted.

For a couple of hours we talked about the Dreamtime world around us. Then Larry announced it was time to eat. The men very carefully cleared the dirt from the sheet of tin and then lifted it away from the pit oven. The smell that wafted up was very appetizing. "This is where you eat and eat," someone told me from the darkness beyond the campfire.

From that fountainhead source called Dreamtime there is also a strict tradition about who receives each portion of meat. Various parts of the body are given to parents and in-laws, brothers, sisters and hunting companions according to custom and tradition regardless of who actually made the kill.

"He that kill 'um should only eat head," said Larry jokingly. "But we're more generous than that to old Jadbula."

Lifting the carcass from the pit, we opened it up with a hatchet and with knives began to carve off pieces of meat. It was absolutely delicious and very clean. The juices that had collected in the animal's chest cavity were seasoned (with a bottle of Worchestershire sauce!) and the resulting soup was soaked up with campfire bread. This tasty mixture was then washed down with tea. This, indeed, was where we ate and ate.

The Settlers from Europe Rename The Game

As mentioned in an earlier chapter, the face of Australia began to be changed by white settlers and their agriculture in the late 18th century. At first, the kangaroo was an important part of the cultural diet, probably because domestic stock was still too valuable to be killed. As the colony became more substantial, however, mutton replaced kangaroo meat on the wealthier farms. By the mid-1800s, eating kangaroo was associated with being a poor farmer.

Bit by bit, the image of the kangaroo as a resource began to change to one of a nuisance. The animals not only damaged crops and fences but competed with domestic stock for precious grass. Kangaroos were no longer a valuable commodity and coursing clubs were formed just for the sport of hunting them from horseback. To aid in the chase, a special swift-running breed of dog with powerful jaws, the kangaroo dog, was developed. For a while, coursing with kangaroo dogs provided local sportsmen with great amusement.

But the realization was growing that agriculture was also benefiting the kangaroo; land clearing and the provisioning of watering places were allowing the animals to multiply in tremendous numbers. By the late 19th century, kangaroos occurred in very high numbers in most of Australia's pastoral areas. In an 1863 editorial, the newspaper *Borderwatch* warned:

> It is becoming daily more apparent that some system of wholesale destruction will have to be devised for checking the rapid increase of kangaroos. So much have these animals increased in late years that if measures are not speedily taken against them, they threaten to overrun the district. At present, they swarm in every part of it. Many of the sheep farmers believe they have nearly as many kangaroos on their runs as sheep. We should therefore preach a crusade against kangaroos.

Coursing was clearly not a viable method for eradicating large numbers of kangaroos. A technique borrowed from the Aborigines, called the "battue," proved to be much more successful. It consisted of an organized roundup of the quarry into a dead-end fence or pit. Once the kangaroos were contained in this small area, they could then be shot or clubbed to death.

For thousands of years, bush fires started and maintained by Aborigines improved and maintained wildlife habitat. Modern wildlife managers are now realizing that this ancient practice is one of the most important management tools at their disposal.

Grazing pressure by kangaroos can have an effect on land that has no hard-hooved domestic stock on it, as evidenced by this fenced enclosure in Cape Gantheaume Conservation Park on Kangaroo Island in southern Australia. Kangaroos were allowed to graze in the right paddock but were excluded from the left one. Although the grass has been nibbled short in this scene, the kangaroos' soft feet have left the plant community and the area's fragile soils intact.

The number of animals killed in this manner was often astonishing. On one property in the state of Victoria, a thousand or so kangaroos were driven into a fenced enclosure in a single day. "Here the animals were met by horsemen armed with waddies (short clubs), who killed five hundred, retired for refreshments and then killed the rest."

With the arrival of white settlers and such slaughter, the Aborigines' attitude toward conservation sometimes changed radically. Perhaps such actions as the destruction of all the wallabies on a certain Great Barrier Reef island and the wanton torching of the landscape can be explained as culture shock from the European invasion. In recent years, however, Aborigines have started to manage their lands with traditional methods again.

Kangaroos were legally declared noxious before the turn of the century under ACT #11.44 VIC 1880. It now became the duty of Australian landowners and leasees to destroy them in order to "protect pastures and livestock." Rural communities went to work at this job with a vengeance. In Queensland, a battue of 12 to 14 people shooting daily killed a total of 20,000 kangaroos in a six-week period. Over the course of a few years, some properties reported destroying between 40,000 and 60,000 kangaroos each. In spite of these high kill numbers, the kangaroo problem continued to grow.

It was from this period in history that many of the current ideas about kangaroos were originally formulated. Many ranchers still believe that a kangaroo will eat as much grass as a sheep. Some even think one can eat as much pasturage as three sheep. It's little wonder that kangaroos came to be regarded as a terrible pestilence that damaged entire crops, destroyed miles of fences, fouled water holes and ate out pastures.

In the past decade a great deal of study has gone into determining what and how much a kangaroo really does eat. The answers have been inconclusive but currently, in scientific circles, it is thought that a large adult kangaroo eats about two-thirds as much forage as a sheep. However, in good seasons with plenty of moisture, there is little dietary overlap between kangaroos and sheep. It's only when times get bad, such as during a drought, that there is any significant competition for the same food plants.

How much damage do kangaroos actually do? The answer is hard to quantify. In the last few years there have been a number of studies that attempt to answer this question. Each of these studies was based on surveys of landholders' perceptions of kangaroo damage. Unfortunately, the bottom line damage values are just guesses and they vary widely. These surveys do serve, however, as good indicators of rural attitudes.

A poll in the Western Division of New South Wales discovered that 68 percent of farmers and graziers regarded kangaroos as their major problem after variability in weather. In another study, 67 percent of interviewed landholders claimed that they did not want kangaroos on their property. These surveys also showed that fence damage by kangaroos is thought to be responsible for some 40 percent of the fencing maintenance costs in pastoral areas. (At regular crossing points, kangaroos prefer to dig under fences rather than to jump over them. They bunch up wire netting and undermine fence posts.)

In 1985, the Commonwealth Scientific and Industrial Research Organization (CSIRO) asked 600 landholders in kangaroo pest districts to estimate the damage caused by these animals. The farmers put the total cost of kangaroo damage to agriculture at more than $113 million (Australian) per year. This figure suggests that kangaroos cause a 10 percent loss in livestock-carrying capacity in these regions. Other more recent studies place the figure closer to $300 million or somewhere between $6 and $20 per kangaroo.

These survey studies can be misleading, though. The polls are taken from people who believe they are being hurt. The reality is not always the same as the perception. Sometimes when damage is attributed to kangaroos, the real culprit may be some other animals or improper land management by the landholders themselves. Unfortunately, these causes are not readily apparent without long and costly research. So, for the moment, in rural Australia it is the landholders' opinions that still determine much of the kangaroo's fate.

"There needs to be a reasonable balance struck," says Bob Miles, a researcher with the Queensland Department of Primary Production. "Kangaroos are a natural

At regular crossing points, kanga-roos prefer to dig under fences rather than jump over them.

animal and they need protecting, but the estimates now indicate that we still have nearly as many kangaroos in southwest Queensland as we have sheep."

One evening at sunset, some 50 miles (80 kilometers) west of the town of Dubbo in New South Wales, a friend and I stopped to set up camp after a long day of cross-country driving. From our tents we could watch a mob of kangaroos feeding in an adjacent oat field. "If these were the only kangaroos in the world," I remember musing, "they would be treasured beyond any king's ransom." But they're not and as I watched them feeding and tramping about, I wondered how I'd feel about their presence if this were my field. Frankly, I don't think I'd like it very much.

CONTROVERSY OVER KANGAROOS

Australia's first conservation society was formed in 1909. It opposed battues but did not object to the destruction of kangaroos by humane means when they were proven to be a problem for farmers and graziers. Although some legislative protection had been extended to kangaroos during Australia's history, it was not until the 1960s that the first real concerns for the kangaroo's future began to be recognized.

Pressure from different conservation, wildlife and animal welfare groups succeeded in getting the government to ban all exports of kangaroo products during this period. (The ban was progressively lifted, state by state, during 1975 and 1976.)

An industry had grown up around the killing of unwanted kangaroos. People, known as shooters, were invited to hunt on properties that carried large numbers and high densities of kangaroos. Instead of wasting the carcasses, as was done during the days of the battue, the hunters now sold skins to tanneries and some of the meat to pet food canners. Until the ban, however, this industry was nearly uncontrolled in its killing and marketing of kangaroos and there was growing widespread concern about the fate of four of the large kangaroo species. Responding to worldwide criticism about kangaroo killing in Australia, the United States placed them on the Endangered Species List. In places as far away as London and New York, people had begun to believe that kangaroos were becoming extinct.

Back in Australia, though, the outback landholders were still facing the same old problem—too many kangaroos overrunning their pastures and croplands. In the interest of agricultural security, something had to be done.

"In 1974, management of kangaroo populations by state wildlife authorities was subjected to critical review and the Commonwealth (federal) Government required that legally harvested animals be identified by a tagging system, that management procedures be documented, and that quotas apply to restrict the total commercial harvest," writes Dr. Gerry Maynes of the Australian National Parks and Wildlife Service. "As those measures were introduced, the ban on exports introduced by the Commonwealth Government was progressively removed." Kangaroo products for export are now controlled by the Australian National Parks and Wildlife Service (a federal organization) through the *Wildlife Protection (Regulation of Exports and Imports) Act.*

Although policy implementation was left to each state, the combined pressures of international criticism and farmers' needs has eventually led to an extremely organized system of kangaroo culling. The prime directive of this system is to control kangaroos as pests while at the same time preserving the viability of each region's kangaroo population. This is a difficult task and, fortunately, it has spawned a great deal of scientific inquiry about how to accomplish it. These objective findings are almost immediately included into each year's management plan. In spite of continuing criticism from conservation and animal rights groups, this new system seems to be working; not one of the affected species seems in any danger of extinction.

A great deal of the public's criticism appears to stem from the idea that kangaroos, which are wild animals, are being commercially exploited. However, in the United States, more than 4 million wild deer are killed annually by sportsmen (who are often inexperienced shooters). The owner of any sporting goods store in this country will gladly tell you that deer hunting is big business.

According to recent figures published by Whitetails Unlimited, a special interest organization for deer hunters, the current deer population in the United States is somewhere close to 23 million animals. Around the turn of the century, unregulated market hunting had severely reduced their numbers to only about 500,000 animals nationwide, less than $1/45$th of their present numbers. Because of wildlife management programs enacted by various government and conservation organizations, they have since more than recovered their original numbers. Like the kangaroo, deer find that the features of rural civilization (roads, pastures, fields, farms and woodlots) have inadvertently combined to create ideal deer habitat.

Although market hunting has been outlawed, recreational harvest levels in some states, such as Texas, Georgia, Minnesota, Wisconsin and Pennsylvania, can run as high as 400,000 deer annually. (The accepted sustained harvest level for deer is usually calculated as 20 to 25 percent of the total population, kangaroos are conservatively rated at about 15 percent.)

There are other, more hidden, wildlife industries here, too. The commercial harvest of raccoons in the U.S. is in excess of 3 million and the North American harvest of Muskrats is estimated to be greater than 7 million animals per year. Surprisingly little controversy has been generated by these "accepted" practices.

Responding to lobbyist and senatorial pressures to renew the ban on importing kangaroo products, in 1990 the United States Fish and Wildlife Service sent a study team to do a field review of the Australian kangaroo management program. Not surprisingly, the American report was quite favorable:

> Due to excellent protective legislation, healthy populations, adequate enforcement and the extensive system of National Parks and preserves, the three (imported) species of kangaroos (Red kangaroo, Western grey kangaroo and Eastern grey kangaroo) are not likely to become endangered within the foreseeable future. Consideration should be given to removing them from the list of threatened species protected by the Endangered Species Act.

These findings may anger some pressure groups but it is a relief to see that there is finally some international recognition of what Australia's cockeys (landholders) have known all along: Kangaroos are not being threatened with extinction by hunting.

THE KANGAROO INDUSTRY

Grinding forward in low gear, the four-wheel drive truck bucks and sways along the dirt track. It is nearly midnight and still another hour until lunchtime. As we bounce on the seat in the truck's cab, Ted Heineman's helper flicks the powerful beam of the roof-mounted spotlight back and forth out across the dark landscape. For an instant, a small tree glows in the light, then a bush, then the forms of three Red kangaroos. The animals scatter and run away as soon as the truck comes to a halt.

"'Roos are very skitterish on windy nights like this," Ted says. "The best times for hunting them are just a day or two before you get rain." Ted Heineman is one of Australia's few full-time professional 'roo shooters.

The flitting spotlight momentarily illuminates three more kangaroos. "Two females and a joey." The truck and the spotlight move on. Another group of six kangaroos are illuminated briefly and then also passed over. Because he is paid by the carcass weight of his quarry, Ted shoots only big males and the very largest females.

Near a line of trees, we see numerous green eyes glowing in the light.

"Sheep!" Ted comments. "We'd best move on. Sheep and 'roos don't like to mix."

A short while later, we see two big male kangaroos. One of them continues to graze while the truck stops and Ted readies the rifle. It is a .225 caliber center-fire mounted with an 8X scope and it looks expensive. In Australia, the average 'roo shooter's gun costs somewhere between $1,800 and $2,000 (Australian).

"Shhhhh . . ." Ted lays the rifle across the padded armrest mounted on the driver's door. An expectant moment passes and then "Bang!" A hit. "Bang!" Another hit. A third animal moves into the line of sight but Ted passes it up. "Too small, we'll let it grow up."

We drive as close to the prostrate forms as we can, then stop and get out of the truck. In the headlights we see them, bleeding, both shot in the head, killed instantly. Like many others, these kills were made at more than 100 yards (91 meters) away. We load the carcasses onto the truck and roll on. There are now 11 dead kangaroos on the truck. All of them have been shot in the head.

This killing leaves me feeling queasy but I am determined to see for myself just what this industry is all about. Most of the shooters that I've been with seem to care about their quarry and all try to be humane by making every shot an instant kill. A thorough professional, Ted has a better than 98 percent accuracy rate.

"I suppose that if I had to be killed," Ted's helper tells me, "then I would prefer that it would be this way. I don't think these kangaroos feel a thing."

A professional shooter loads dressed kangaroo carcasses onto his truck.

A shooter usually loads six to a dozen 'roos on his truck before he stops on an open clay pan to skin and dress them. Like any slaughter, this is gruesome business.

Ted takes a moment to grab a bite and to talk, via two-way radio, to another shooter working somewhere else in the night. He says he's having a good evening with over 60 kangaroos already on the truck.

Ted says he'll have to bag about 20 'roos tonight just to make expenses for the effort. Each bullet costs him from 20 to 25 cents, and then there's fuel and maintenance for the truck (flat tires from the rough country are a big problem), and gear and food. At today's prices, a single kangaroo does not count for very much against these expenses.

"Last year I shot about 8,000 'roos," Ted tells me. "That brought in a gross of something around $40,000, but then I had to deduct my expenses from that. We're not getting rich doing this but, still, we're making a living." A friend of his, who shot over 12,000 kangaroos last year, just bought a new $30,000 truck. (The average 'roo shooter's truck costs between $25,000 and $30,000.)

At least 70 percent of the approximately 1,600 registered kangaroo shooters in Australia have an additional source of income. Some have part-time jobs during the day or shoot only on weekends. Others move over to better paying targets, such as feral pigs, when they are abundant and the market prices good.

Today, the number of kangaroos a shooter can kill each year is strictly limited by a quota system based on population estimates from aerial surveys. Like most shooters, Ted Heineman selects less than 5 percent of the kangaroos that he spots. Taking small kangaroos that weigh under 26.5 pounds (12 kilograms) is just not economical. At current market prices, a 44-pound {20-kilo) dressed kangaroo carcass is only worth around $6 (Australian) to the shooter.

In order to be able to deliver their nightly harvest at sunrise, most commercial shooters operate within 60 miles (100 kilometers) of a town having a processing center and the effort is only economical while kangaroos are abundant. When their tallies drop to an uneconomical level, most shooters will move to another area. Failing that, they will often take up other work.

The unlicensed "weekend shooter," on the other hand, is not constrained by such economic considerations. These people, who usually drive out from the cities, shoot kangaroos just for target practice. The kills are usually illegal and the animals are just left in the field to rot. It's obvious these people have little regard for wildlife or the waste of an economic resource. There is no record of how many kangaroos are killed this way, but one nationwide estimate put the number into the millions. I met a man in Queensland who bragged about shooting 150 kangaroos in a single weekend. This kind of irresponsibility is abhorred by the professional shooter.

The Industry's Early Days

Kangaroo parts have been a commercial commodity since Australia's early colonial days. In 1802, the governor of New South Wales put a landing tax on the export of kangaroo skins but major exploitation didn't really get under way until the 1850s. By 1923, more than 300,000 kangaroo skins were being trafficked each year just through the city of Brisbane alone. When refrigeration became economically feasible in the 1950s, trade in kangaroo meat began in earnest.

No one will ever know how many animals were killed during the early days of the kangaroo industry since they were generally regarded as little more than living vermin with useful hides. However, between 1877 and 1906, when Queensland had a bounty on dead kangaroos, over 20 million payments were made. (This works out to an average of about 660,000 animals per year during this 30-year period.) Fortunately, the overall effect on Queensland's population of large kangaroos seems to have been negligible.

Pages 144–45: Kangaroo shooters line up at a New South Wales buying station in order to sell the previous night's harvest.

Kangaroo skins being salted and baled for shipment overseas.

The Kangaroo Market Today

Skins destined to become leather are still the most valued product in the kangaroo industry. However, because of rising labor costs, there are only a few tanneries left in Australia. Most of the 'roo skins are dehaired and "pickled" with chemical preservatives. Then they are shipped overseas to other countries. Most major buyers are in Germany, Italy and Japan. The furry, cuddly toys, such as souvenir koalas, are among the few items still manufactured in Australia from kangaroo skins.

A professional skin shooter may stay out in the field five or six weeks before returning to town with his harvest. Every day, each new skin is cleaned and carefully salted. (An efficient operator can take and prepare as many as 2,000 skins in one trip.) Unfortunately, some Australian states, such as Queensland, do not require that the entire kangaroo carcass be utilized. In these areas, nearly half of the animals that are shot are simply wasted and left to rot. Bullet holes do not downgrade a skin that will be used for leather.

Kangaroo leather is soft, extremely durable and "breathes" well. It is particularly popular in the manufacture of athletic shoes but is also used to make ordinary shoes, wallets, belts and sporting goods such as golf bags, steering wheel covers and bicycle seats. Most of the 1 or 2 million kangaroo skins tanned in Italy each year are used in the domestic shoe market but no one knows (or is telling) just how many of these items end up being exported around the world. At the point of sale, most products made from kangaroo skins are not labeled as such. I am almost certain that my favorite pair of running shoes is made from kangaroo but there is no tag that states it as a fact.

The kangaroo industry took only skins until the 1950s, when a disease called myxomatosis greatly reduced Australia's rabbit population. Butchers and pet food processors quickly turned to kangaroo meat as a substitute.

Most kangaroo meat still is marketed as pet food but there is a growing demand for its use by people. In contrast to beef or mutton, kangaroo meat contains very little visible fat and, in fact, is very lean and tasty. One study found that kangaroo meat averaged less than 2 percent fat and contained almost no cholesterol. Advocates call it "the red meat that is good for you to eat." In a paper published in the August 1988 issue of the *Australian Zoologist*, Kerin O'Dea, professor of human nutrition at Victoria's Deakin University offers this insight on the benefits of eating kangaroo and other wild meat:

> Although Aborigines develop high frequencies of obesity, diabetes, and diseases of the cardio-vascular system when they are living in an urban environment, there is *no* evidence that they suffered from these conditions when they lived as hunter-gatherers. Indeed, we have shown that when urbanized Aborigines returned temporarily to their hunter-gatherer lifestyle, there are significant reductions in risk factors for diabetes and heart disease in non-diabetic subjects and marked improvement in the metabolic abnormalities associated with these diseases.

(Of course, the hunter-gatherer lifestyle also offers a great deal of healthful exercise and companionship.)

Kangaroo meat is leaner than rabbit and chicken breast and contains a total fat content similar to Whiting (a fish). By contrast, a T-bone beef steak can be up to 9 or 10 percent fat. No other red meat even comes close to kangaroo, from a nutritional point of view, and researchers have shown it is consistently freer from disease than domestic livestock.

Unfortunately, some Australian states do not allow the sale of kangaroo meat for human consumption. It is legal, however, in Tasmania, South Australia, the Northern Territory and the national capital territory encompassing Canberra. Here you can find kangaroo fillets at the meat counter in supermarkets and on the menu in many popular restaurants.

Other states will probably soon follow this lead. In New South Wales, the process of legalizing kangaroo meat for human consumption has already begun. Apparently this move has been led by Sydney restaurateurs who receive numerous inquiries from visiting Japanese and Americans wanting to try a bit of kangaroo. A similar move in Queensland was recently blocked by the cattlemen's union.

Some kangaroo meat is exported from Australia, mostly for pet food. Tommy Thompson, a kangaroo meat processor in Sydney, sells a lot of meat to Japanese zoos.

"All of the meat that goes overseas goes frozen," he says. "We're doing about 1,500 carcasses per week."

Europe is also a big destination for frozen kangaroo meat, especially Germany, France, Spain and the United Kingdom. Once it enters Europe's protein-hungry markets, it is very difficult to trace where the meat goes. Commonly, the meat is minced up for sausages or resold as venison. In either case, it is no longer identified as kangaroo.

Other important buyers of kangaroo meat include Norway, Papua New Guinea, Indonesia and the United States. During a recent visit to Malaysia, I noticed a street vendor advertising mutton from Australia. When I examined his meat, I soon realized that it was not mutton at all. There is only one animal in the world that produces haunches the size and shape of what he was selling: a kangaroo.

The Quota System

"The current system of kangaroo management in Australia varies to some extent between each state," says Gerry Maynes, director of the Australian National Parks and Wildlife Service's wildlife monitoring unit. "Every state in Australia must adhere to a commercial harvest quota that is set to prevent the demand for kangaroo products leading to an overharvest. We see the kangaroo industry as a controlled management tool which operates to provide damage mitigation for the landholders."

Each year the number of kangaroos to be culled is set by a special advisory committee comprised of people representing the interests of the state National Parks and Wildlife Services, the National Farmer's Federation and a number of other rural interest groups including the Australian Rangelands Society, the Ecological Society of Australia and various animal rights and conservation groups. Every state receives a specific allocation.

The criteria that determine each state's quota is drawn from population estimates done by aerial and ground surveys. The species composition, sizes and sex ratios of recently harvested kangaroos and local seasonal conditions are also part of this formula. Together, these factors provide the basis for an estimate of the current "standing population." At present, Australia's population of large kangaroos is considerably more than 20 million animals. In 1983 the population was around 13 million. During the quota-setting process, farmer's representatives are asked for advice on local kangaroo populations. Problem zones are allocated a higher proportion of the quota than are other areas but in every case the welfare of the total population is kept in mind.

"A general rule of thumb for a safe harvest level is about 15 percent of the estimated population," says Gerry Maynes. "There is some suggestion that in the case of Red kangaroos we may be able to take around 20 percent."

Currently, these quotas affect only five species of kangaroos: the Red kangaroo, the Eastern grey kangaroo, the Western grey kangaroo, the Common wallaroo and the Whiptail wallaby. These are the so-called "commercial" kangaroos. Five other species of macropods are considered pests in some areas but they have limited commercial interest. These animals are usually shot by the landholder himself.

A great deal of controversy has erupted over the steady growth of the kangaroo culling quotas. In 1975, slightly more than 1 million kangaroos were available for commercial harvest. In 1983, more than 3 million animals were legally available and by 1989, that total had increased beyond 5.5 million kangaroos. In the past few years, the quota's growth seems to have leveled off around the 5 million mark.

Since it is government policy to ensure, whenever possible, that culled 'roos are taken by the kangaroo industry, some conservationists are charging that the primary reason that kangaroos are killed today is because of their commercial value. These critics assert that there is simply not enough data to substantiate the need to kill kangaroos. For example, the bulk of the kangaroo kill is done in the semi-arid rangelands of Australia's interior but only about 10 percent of that country's sheep and cattle occur within the bounds of these commercial killing zones. As animal rights activist Peter Rawlinson points out, the kangaroo industry can only claim to be assisting 10 percent of Australia's grazing stock.

One organization, Greenpeace, argues that continued commercial killing may ultimately threaten kangaroos with extinction.

"It is our understanding that the ranges of even the common species of kangaroo have become much restricted to what they used to be," Molly Olson, director of the Sydney Greenpeace office, told me during an interview. "The numbers may have increased in some areas . . . so that there may even be as many as there were 200 years ago, but they are now living in a much more confined area."

If there is an environmental collapse in these reduced areas, it is possible that the kangaroos could be wiped out. However, as important as this concerned speculation for the future may be, there are many more immediate voices that must be heard by government.

"I want to impress upon you why we want the industry to continue," says Bill Bonthrone, manager of Ingaby Station in southeastern Queensland and president of the United Grazier's Association of Queensland and the National Farmers Federation.

"If it should end, it means we farmers will have to do the culling. And if I'm forced to do it, the day will come when I won't shoot them. With kangaroo numbers increasing like they are, I'll be forced to poison them. That's just how serious the situation is. You just can't have a crop that's worth $50,000 wiped out by kangaroos and expect to survive."

The Grigg Proposal

Professor Gordon Grigg of the University of Queensland in Brisbane has been looking long and hard at the kangaroo problem from an unusual vantage point—the pilot's seat of a low-flying aircraft—and he may have come up with a viable solution.

Each year he takes part in the aerial survey that helps determine the current population of kangaroos in semi-arid Australia. Piloting the high-winged Cessna, Grigg flies just 250 feet above the ground along a series of predetermined transects that make up a particular survey block. Two trained observers sitting in the plane's back seat scan a 200-meter-wide strip of ground on either side of the plane.

I recently flew with the survey team as it buzzed over central Australia. At first I saw nothing but bushes and dry stream-courses below . . . even when an animal was pointed out to me. At such low altitude, our speed of 100 knots didn't allow me much time to search a particular spot.

Within 20 minutes, though, I was beginning to recognize a few animals here and there: goats, sheep, cattle, rabbits, emus. "Look! There's one . . . two . . . three . . . four . . . five kangaroos down there. How many did you gentlemen see?"

"Twenty-two."

These guys were good. They had trained for over two years before qualifying for the job. Yet, depending on the terrain, even they can spot only about one-half or so of the animals actually down there. Later, the survey results, complete with sighting correction factors, will be scaled into a population model for the entire area.

"After more than a decade of flying these low-level surveys over the eastern two-thirds of Australia," says Dr. Grigg, "the strongest impression I am left with is the huge impact that the hard-hooved, hard-feeding sheep have had on the landscape. It is difficult to find a scene where the imprint of hooves is not clearly visible. The vegetation has been ground underfoot, exposing the fragile soil, changing its drainage properties and lessening its suitability for plant growth."

Kangaroos, on the other hand, have soft feet that do not harm tender vegetation. This can be an important factor in the revegetation of an area.

"Land degradation has been identified as the number-one rural problem in Australia," Grigg continued. "Almost 2 million square kilometers (772,200 square miles) of the arid zone (about 55 percent) has been seriously degraded. Much of this area is at risk of becoming permanent desert."

The obvious way to address the problem is by reducing the number of sheep and cattle on the land. But how? Economic pressure has pushed a lot of graziers' backs to the wall. Many are trying to survive by putting more stock on the already flogged and depleted land. It's a vicious cycle in which, sooner or later, everyone will be the loser.

"Kangaroos thrive in unnaturally high numbers on these same lands, where they are regarded as pests," says Professor Grigg. "Kangaroo meat has great potential for sale at high prices, yet graziers are grateful when the kangaroo shooter comes to take the carcasses away.

"In a nutshell, my idea is that we should undertake a marketing drive for kangaroo products, raising the price to such an extent that graziers will find it worthwhile to reduce their traditional hard-footed stock in favor of free-range kangaroos. In turn, the reduction of sheep numbers would help halt land degradation." A well-run national marketing campaign could produce an increased demand by simply alerting consumers to the health benefits of kangaroo meat: Save Your Heart. Save The Land. Eat Kangaroo. (Remember, kangaroo meat contains less than 2 percent fat and almost no cholesterol.)

"If kangaroos are worth a lot of money," says Dr. Grigg, "it's going to be in the property owner's best interest not to take more animals than he thinks his land can support because he'll want to harvest some the next year and the next. . . ."

If Professor Grigg's idea becomes implemented, the kangaroo industry's management would probably become similar to that of a commercial fishery. Kangaroos could not be owned by individuals, like domestic animals, but would be managed and harvested as a natural resource in areas and on properties where they occurred in sufficient numbers.

The Grigg Proposal, as it is publicly referred to, has met extremely mixed and vociferous reviews. In the long run, the idea's success hinges on some rather fundamental changes in attitude that could reshape Australia's view of itself and its wildlife.

Opposite: An aerial view of the sheep rangelands of Australia showing soil damage trails created by hard-hooved stock converging on a watering point.

Kangaroos and people can coexist. In Woodgate, Queensland, the townsfolk have voted to include kangaroos in the city. The free-ranging animals are now an important tourist attraction to the area.

Some critics say that the rural community is much too conservative to try such an unusual thing as kangaroo "ranching." Yet the country's sheep industry is in economic crisis and may soon fail in many regions. Other folks abhor the idea of eating their national symbol but then seem to forget that millions of the animals are killed each year simply as pests.

"If all the kangaroos that are culled each year were sold as supermarket specialty meat, it would represent less than 3 percent of this country's entire meat budget," Dr. Grigg told me. "It's not like it would flood the economy."

There is a cacophony of arguments to dismiss Grigg's idea. But somehow it keeps bouncing back into public view again and again. Kangaroos evolved on this land and are finely tuned to its seasonal changes. However reluctantly, change *is* coming; one Australian newspaper headline that recently caught my eye shouted "EATING ROOS WILL SAVE THEM: Govt." Perhaps the kangaroo's economic and soil conservation value may soon be realized and its status as a nuisance put to an end.

Opposite: A golfer at the Anglesea Golf Course in Victoria plays through an unusual hazard, a mob of kangaroos.

WHITHER WE GO?:

Current Research and Future Hopes

Although they are considered pests by Australia's agricultural establishment, kangaroos have long held an honored position in the national conscience. They are the living symbol of the country, appearing on its coat of arms and its money. In the public's mind, the land and its kangaroos are almost synonymous and it is difficult to find a person there who doesn't harbor strong feelings about both of them.

There is no doubt that kangaroos occupy a unique love/hate position in Australian culture. This fact was driven home, time after time, when I interviewed landholders about their kangaroo culling programs. One rancher located in the heart of the kangaroo "pest" district of southwest Queensland expressed this feeling most succinctly:

"Yes, I have shooters on my property almost every night because these 'roos are getting completely out of hand . . . it's getting to be like a plague around here," he told me. "On the other hand, if they were totally removed from my place I'd even be more upset. I only want to control their numbers, not eliminate them entirely. Hell, to be perfectly honest, Mate, I'm rather fond of the damned things."

This fondness has also been the driving force behind "Skippy," a popular children's television program about a boy and his pet kangaroo. A kind of Australian "Lassie," Skippy is the clever animal hero of numerous adventures involving the boy and his national parks ranger dad. "Skippy" is also one of the country's longest-running television series. For more than 20 years "Skippy" has been helping to mould Australian children's perceptions of kangaroos and other wildlife in a positive way.

"It's had a very strong influence," says Chris Bryant, a professional kangaroo shooter in New South Wales who is concerned about the growing tide of criticism towards his industry. "The kids who watched the program as they grew up are now 25 and 30 years old, yet they still relate back to that small kangaroo of their childhood . . . it's not an image that is easy to get rid of."

It's a viewpoint that seems to be slowly changing the way kangaroos are being regarded in this country and I can foresee an upgrade in the legal status of these animals in the near future. Presently they are considered both protected wildlife and pests.

Opposite: A shotgun-blasted road sign seems to symbolize Australia's love/hate relationship with kangaroos.

Advertising and television are having a great effect in changing the public's image of kangaroos.

A similar metamorphosis occurred in the early 1970s in the United States when the American black bear (*Ursus americanis*), previously thought of as a nuisance predator, became a big game animal. That single change has led to an increased interest in bears and vastly more effective conservation programs for the species. A similar action would also benefit kangaroos, even *if* the commercial industry were allowed to continue. As Professor Grigg predicts, the kangaroo would become much more valuable in everyone's mind.

MORE NEW APPROACHES

"A lot of scientists in Australia rely on the kangaroo industry to provide them with their living," Michael Kennedy told me in a crowded Sydney lunch bar. "You see, every year the Feds need biologists to provide facts and figures to determine the culling and export quotas for 'roo skins. Unfortunately, we can get very few of these biologists to study the small and medium-sized marsupials simply because they are not economically important and therefore no money is available to study them."

Kennedy is working with the World Wildlife Fund to develop a comprehensive action plan for Austral-Asian marsupials. A first for Australia, this blueprint will help guide research for these animals' conservation future. It will also be a tool to help secure funding for study of the many "overlooked" species. (The World Wildlife Fund is actually a branch of the IUCN or International Union for Conservation of Nature. Although it maintains and publishes the *Red Data* books that monitor the status of threatened animals around the world, the central purpose of the IUCN is to help nations take advantage of natural resources without destroying any that are irreplaceable.)

"We see a need to manage land by bio-regions," Mr. Kennedy continued. "We also wish to see a system of management by task forces implemented across the country . . . so that we have the National Park Service, the Water Board, the Forest Commission and various farmers and miners all taking part in developing regional action plans. In order to work, a task force must consist of the people who have control of the land in a particular region. Within each task force we also envision a recovery team that will do the actual hands-on work."

"We do need a fresh approach to land management," echoes Rick Humphries, a lobbyist for Greenpeace-Australia. "The next generation of outback station (ranch) managers will be different; they'll be dropping long-held assumptions and asking more appropriate questions about how to protect their land and conserve its resources."

Wildlife Sanctuaries and National Parks

One of the best ways to safeguard wildlife and their habitats is to formally secure these important lands as forest reserves, wildlife sanctuaries or national parks. Fortunately, since the 1960s, the Australian government has taken a lead in acquiring new land for these purposes. In 1983 it reported that 116,000 square miles (approximately 300,000 square kilometers) had been protected in this manner. By 1988 the amount of protected area had grown by almost 40,000 square miles (to approx 400,000 square kilometers). Today, nearly 5.5 percent of Australia has been set aside primarily for the conservation of nature. When added up, this represents an area that is one and a half times as large as Italy.

Although the percentage of protected lands seems to be steadily increasing, there are critical habitats, such as rainforests, that seem almost totally lacking in effective guardianship. The continued logging of certain rainforest remnants in Queensland,

Jack Higgins, caretaker of Pebbly Beach Campground, south of Sydney, has been hand-feeding wild kangaroos for many years. These tame Eastern grey kangaroos are both a delight to tourists and a great opportunity for naturalists studying animal behavior.

New South Wales and Tasmania has generated deep divisions and a vocal controversy within Australian society. I can only hope that when resolution finally comes there are enough large tracts of these old-growth forests still standing to even matter.

There are other ways that land can be retained as wildlife habitat. Those unused "back sections" of farms and ranches often have important wildlife values. Colonies of endangered rock-wallabies, for instance, have been discovered living in seldom-visited rock piles on private property.

Another important habitat, as far as kangaroos are concerned, is a public right-of-way system known as the stock routes. Stock routes are broad avenues reserved for driving sheep and cattle from one area to another in order to reach new pastures or rail connections to city markets.

The moving herds are colorful sights, reminiscent of the old American West, with drovers on horseback (or motorbikes) waving and whistling to keep the animals moving. They are usually accompanied by that ever-watchful working dog, the Australian shepherd, which rushes here and there to round up any strays.

"These stock routes are really quite an extensive maze," says Bob Miles, land resource manager with the Queensland Department of Primary Industry. "There are thousands of kilometers of them, many up to 2 kilometers (1.25 miles) wide, following drainage areas and running across properties and connecting all of the major centers in a region. Although they're indicated on national maps, they're not marked in a way that a person who is not a drover would find them."

"Graziers can graze their stock on these routes but they cannot make improvements or do any clearing," continues Mr. Miles. "Kangaroo shooting is also not allowed. Because of these protections, stock routes have become important interconnecting wildlife habitats and kangaroo migration corridors."

Island Refuges

For some kangaroo species, offshore island refuges have become critical for their continued existence. Although these islands are often very limited in area, they provide a great deal of security from invasion by predators from the mainland. The surrounding water creates an effective "moat" that isolates resident wildlife populations from upsetting disturbances.

Bernier and Dorre islands off Western Australia, for example, now provide extremely important refuges for three macropod species. One species, the Rufous hare-wallaby (*Lagorchestes hirsutus*), was once abundant throughout the interior of Western Australia. It is now restricted to these islands and to two small colonies in the Tanami Desert of the Northern Territory. Another species, the Banded hare-wallaby (*Lagostrophus facsiatus*), occurs only on these two islands. There are efforts underway to reintroduce it to nearby Dirk Hartog Island. The Burrowing bettong (*Bettongia lesusur*), the third species, is fortunately present on several other small islands.

The island of Tasmania harbors two unique macropod species, the Tasmanian pademelon (*Thylogale billardierii*) and the Tasmanian bettong (*Bettongia giamardi*). Both species were once widespread and plentiful but have become extinct on the mainland in the last century.

Island sanctuaries can be easily compromised by human interference. The casual release of a pet cat (especially a pregnant one), introduction of pigs or goats, or just rats escaping from a ship can have devastating effects on the native wildlife population on a small island. The smaller the land mass is, the more vulnerable it becomes. For protection to be adequate it is often necessary to restrict and "quarantine" human visitation to these places.

Opposite: Maria Island National Park, near the eastern coast of Tasmania, serves as an outer island refuge for several varieties of Tasmanian macropods.

Because of an island's limited size, even an endangered species may have overpopulation problems. Consider what happened on Maria Island National Park off Tasmania's southeast coast:

A former prison colony, Maria Island itself consists of two land masses connected by a narrow "waist" of land. The widest part of the island is about seven miles (11 km) east to west and its greatest length is about 12.5 miles (20 kilometers).

At present, there are five species of macropods living on the island: the Forester kangaroo (*Macropus giganteus*), which is considered a Tasmanian subspecies of the Eastern grey kangaroo; the Bennett's wallaby (*Macropus rufogriseus*), a Tasmanian subspecies of the Red-necked wallaby; the Tasmanian pademelon (*Thylogale billarierii*); the Long-nosed potoroo (*Potorous tridactylus*); and the Tasmanian bettong (*Bettongia gaimardi*). Only the pademelon and potoroo occur naturally on the island. The other three species were brought to the island in the late 1960s and early 1970s.

At the time, it was thought that the places where these species lived on the mainland of Tasmania were becoming threatened by increased farming and urban expansion. Maria Island was seen as a safe haven for their continued survival. The plan backfired in an unexpected way. The kangaroos actually benefited from the extra food provided by Tasmanian farming and forestry activities and their numbers have increased to the point that population control is required to reduce conflict with agriculture. In retrospect, it never was necessary to move any kangaroos to Maria Island.

Out on Maria Island the transplanted animals also flourished, to the point where overcrowding had increased the mortality rate and incidence of disease.

"It started about five years ago, which would have been about 14 or 15 years after the Forester kangaroos were introduced to Maria Island," says Greg Hocking, a Tasmanian government biologist. "After their populations built up to the carrying capacity of the island, we started to have symptoms of overcrowding such as gut parasites that were killing the younger part of the population. For several years we had a nearly 100-percent mortality rate with yearling Forester kangaroos and Bennett's wallabies."

Because of public pressure, the state was forced to develop a culling program on the island that required rangers to shoot any animals that showed signs of sickness.

"The problem has now largely disappeared but it will recur if we get some good seasons followed by dry years and a shortage of food," adds Hocking.

Tasmania's Controversial 1080 Program

There are five species of macropod marsupials in Tasmania. Of these, two (the Bennett's wallaby and Tasmanian pademelon) are regularly killed for commercial, recreational and crop-protection purposes.

Unlike mainland Australia, Tasmania has an established system of poisoning macropods for "agricultural protection." (Western Australia poisoned kangaroos in the 1950s and many states still use poison to kill Dingoes, feral pigs and rabbits.) The poison of preference is a white, odorless, tasteless power called sodium monofluoroacetate, commonly known as Compound 1080. Developed originally in 1944 in the United States as a rat poison, 1080 soon became famous for its effectiveness as a pest control.

In Tasmania, 1080 was first used as rabbit poison. The shift to poisoning macropods came with the development of forest plantations. Over 30 percent of Tasmania's total area contains forests of potential commercial quality and most of this area is regarded as macropod habitat. According to forest industry sources, somewhere between one-third and one-half of all tree seedlings on forest plantations are damaged by these animals.

"To administer 1080, the foresters usually dig ditches and fill them with carrots and other veggies," says Jenny Sielhorst of "Animal Rescue" in Tasmania. "The animals are allowed to have a few free meals at first, then the carrots are poisoned."

The toxin is also delivered in another method called "one-shot oats." Enough 1080 is put into a gram of oats to kill several wallabies and then, because the substance is highly soluble and soon leaches out in damp weather, it's covered with a kind of plastic coating.

How many animals are killed by 1080 is a matter of conjecture. "The foresters and farmers are supposed to pick up the left-over poisoned carrots and all carcasses," says Sielhorst, "but they don't, even though they will tell you that they do." (Because it may take up to seven days for an animal to die, it is practically impossible to collect all of the poisoned carcasses.)

Since dogs and cats and other animals are very sensitive to 1080, there is also a risk of secondary poisoning from uncollected carcasses. Studies have shown that just one poisoned rabbit can kill 11 dogs or 17 cats. Unfortunately, Tasmania's native carnivores and scavengers run a similar risk.

Some researchers say that the animals killed by 1080 do not feel any pain but this is really not known. In general, the toxin affects an animal's cardiac or nervous system. An affected wallaby may sit hunched, shivering and shaking, for several hours. Then, just before it dies, it will fall to the ground and make running motions with its hind legs and froth at the mouth. If it is male, often its last act will be to ejaculate just before death.

This method of dying is a particularly gruesome sight to contemplate, but there have been several human cases of 1080 poisoning that were not fatal. Although the victims exhibited severe epileptic-like convulsions, as well as cardiac effects, no pain was ever reported. However, some animal species may be more sensitive to pain than we are.

"I can see 1080 poison being phased out in Tasmania through public pressure," says wildlife biologist Greg Hocking. "It will happen . . . it's only a matter of *when* it will happen; whether in the next year because of a new minister that is sympathetic . . . or in ten years from external public pressure."

"We need to look into alternatives such as fencing to help farmers overcome these problems," adds Hocking. "For example, where you have high value crops, it's worth it to spend money on an effective electric fence, particularly for tree crops that represent a considerable investment. Rather than having to resort to poisoning, a fence can effectively protect trees for four or five years until they get above the height of browsing wallabies."

Feral Animal Control

In wildlife management terms, a feral animal is a species that has been introduced, either intentionally or by accident, to a region or continent that is not within its historical range and has subsequently established a breeding population in the wild. Some feral animals are rather benign and do not upset the ecological balance of their new homes. Chinese ring-necked pheasants, for example, have successfully colonized most of western and central North America with no pronounced impact on pre-existing wildlife. The wild horse or mustang of the plains of the far western United States has also been integrated with little overall upset. In contrast, many of Australia's feral mammals species (goats, pigs, cats and foxes) have been extremely damaging to native wildlife populations. Feral animals are accused of direct involvement in the extermination of 45 species of native Australian fauna—mammals, reptiles and birds—in the past 200 years. In the case of smaller macropods, the fox seems to be the worst culprit. (See chapter 4.)

Michael Kennedy is particularly concerned about the problem with foxes.

"We have a situation where foxes have spread almost across the entire country," he says. "Each year they advance farther and farther north into the tropics, farther into the temperate zones and deeper into the deserts. In Australia's arid zones, almost 90 percent of all small-to-medium-sized mammals, including macropods, are either endangered or extinct. We're in a crisis situation."

On May 7, 1988, 47 rare Parma wallabies (*Macropus parma*) were released 75 miles (120 kilometers) south of Sydney in the region where they were first recorded nearly 200 years earlier. The original native population has since vanished. By releasing these captive-reared animals, it was hoped that the species would reestablish itself back in its natural habitat.

By mid-June, however, the last of the animals that had been fitted with radio transmitters had been killed by foxes. Ironically, in preparation of the Parma's repatriation, the local foxes had been so heavily hunted and baited with poison, that rangers believed the predator had been eradicated from the area. Obviously the persistence of this predator had been underestimated.

Dr. Jack Kinnear, senior research scientist at the Department of Conservation and Land Management in Western Australia thinks that foxes are also responsible for the recent extinction of rock-wallabies on an island near Port Hedland on the northwestern coast.

"A study conducted in 1962 reported that the rock-wallaby was very numerous on the island, but today there are none left," he said in a recent newspaper interview. "Foxes do so well because they are environmental generalists and are completely adaptable. At the moment it is possible to control their numbers through poison baits, but that is only a holding measure."

Some Australian conservationists are beginning to believe it is too late to save most of the unique wildlife species that have become easy meals for the quick and deadly fox. The game is not over, though:

"The Australian government has recently coughed up one-half of a million dollars to fund a new CSIRO (Commonwealth Scientific and Industrial Research Organisation) project to find a bio-control for foxes," says Michael Kennedy. "It might eventually take 10 years and 100 million dollars but we've got no choice; we can shoot, trap and poison until we're blue in the face and we'll still have a problem with foxes."

ROAD-KILLED KANGAROOS

One evening as photographer Mark Newman and I were driving back to a campground where we were staying, we turned a corner and ran smack into a wallaby. Stopping the vehicle, we could hear the animal thrashing around underneath the floor. When I backed the car up, a rather dazed kangaroo got to its feet and gained enough composure to hop to the side of the road. A few minutes later it hopped away into the bushes seemingly unharmed. Barring any internal injuries or the development of delayed shock syndrome, this was a lucky brush with death for the kangaroo and, possibly, for us. A week later I learned of an accident that killed a woman and her child when their car collided head-on with a large kangaroo.

Road-kills are a significant mortality factor for at least a dozen kangaroo species. It is such a frequent occurrence in many localities that drivers in these areas must reinforce the front ends of their vehicles with heavy pipe-and-steel mesh grills, called "'roo bars," to prevent serious damage during a collision. Even large trucks have elaborate steel screens erected in front of their radiator grills. Drivers still must remain alert though, especially at night, when a 150-pound kangaroo might

suddenly land in front of the vehicle at the end of a 20-foot leap. Even when equipped with a 'roo bar, there is nothing pleasant about hitting such an animal at 60 miles per hour (100 kilometers per hour).

For tourists driving the long roads across Australia, road-killed macropods are often the only kangaroos they ever get to see, unless they are unlucky enough to hit one themselves. In order to keep myself occupied on lengthy driving trips, I would often conduct informal surveys of road-kill along the way. This kind of survey is actually a good indicator of local population densities because the more numerous a species is, the more they seem to turn up as road-kill.

In the 120 miles (195 kilometers) of nearly straight road from Wilcannia to Broken Hill, New South Wales, we counted 90 dead kangaroos, two dead emus, three dead sheep, one dead cockatoo and three dead Holdens (a popular Australian automobile). Another 115-mile (184-kilometer) trip from Charleville to Mitchell, Queensland, yielded 282 dead 'roos. Some areas along the way would have no dead kangaroos for several miles and then suddenly there would be one spaced every few feet.

A study by G. M. Coulson in Victoria found that kangaroo road-kills tend to peak during certain seasons and that most of them occur around the time of the full moon. He also discovered that the majority of kills were of adult males, "indicating that motor vehicles act as a selective mortality factor."

Posting warning signs where kangaroos are likely to cross roads has had little effect in road-kill rates across the continent and new, more effective measures are currently being sought. In Darwin, for example, where wild wallabies frequenting a city park have become an important tourist attraction, speed bumps installed in key locations have helped cut wallaby deaths from an average of about 40 per month to 15 per month.

A sight that is all too common along the highways of Australia.

A row of automobiles fitted with 'roo bars. The bars help limit damage to the vehicles during collisions with kangaroos on the roadway.

THE SHU-ROO INVENTION

The most unlikely people sometimes become the greatest benefactors of wildlife. One of those people is David Gore, who now resides in Brisbane. David used to go out and shoot kangaroos for sport on the weekends.

"I would never do that now," he said. "I guess I've become much more of a conservationist than I would have ever dreamed. The last thing I ever want to see is a kangaroo shot."

When David got into the business of real-estate development, he had to go on the road and do a lot of selling.

"It was not unusual to travel 1,000 kilometers (600 miles) in a day between one sale and the next," he recalls. "I used to do the driving in the nighttime because I could fill the useless time when other people were asleep."

"I drove a fairly big car, with lots of lights and a heavy-duty 'roo bar on the front. I was buying the best 'roo bars I could but after one or two hits they still would get bent and I would have to throw them away. It was more than a nuisance because each 'roo bar was costing me around $400 to $500. Even with a new one installed on the car, if you hit the kangaroo at the wrong angle, it would still go through your radiator."

"Then one night I tried blowing the car horn every five seconds. It drove me nuts, but it worked! At that point I remembered those ultrasonic dog whistles that people couldn't hear and wondered if something similar would work with kangaroos."

Several electronics inventors joined Mr. Gore's project and helped him to develop a special speaker that looks a bit like a rocket nose-cone with the amazing capability to produce 130 decibels of sound, about three times the level of a police siren. Gore then fitted a bumper-mounted device with three of these speakers and hooked them up to an electronic frequency modulator. It worked! The high-energy, ultra-sonic device was scaring kangaroos away from oncoming cars.

After several years of developing and testing his device, at a cost of some $600,000 to $700,000, David Gore has now begun manufacturing these devices for sale to the public. Sold under the brand name Shu-Roo, Gore's invention is a very promising step towards stopping the senseless slaughter of wildlife on the highway. The biggest hurdle Mr. Gore still faces in getting his product universally accepted is to overcome the buyers' natural sales resistance to "new-fangled" devices by satisfactorily answering that perennial question: "Does it work?"

A letter of testimony from a nationwide car-rental service, Budget Rent-A-Car, seems very encouraging:

> We have had "Shu-Roo" fitted on a variety of our vehicles for the last two years. During this period these vehicles have traveled more than 500,000 kilometers (310,000 miles) between them . . . The accident rate for these vehicles has been reduced by 70% but more importantly, the dollar value of each accident has reduced by 90%. Our major accidents involving kangaroos have been with vehicles *not* fitted with "Shu-Roo."

Extensive tests of his device have convinced David Gore that ultrasonic sound can have other wildlife applications, such as keeping kangaroos away from crop-land. His latest invention, the Roo-Guard, consists of four waterproof speaker stations set on posts 820 feet (250 meters) apart. Powered by a 12-volt car battery, the combined unit will protect 0.6 mile (1 kilometer) of fence line from marauding kangaroos.

"The pulsating beat of the Roo-Guard, which emits a high-frequency sound within the kangaroo's hearing range, causes the animal discomfort, so it naturally

David Gore displays his Shu-Roo invention.

moves away from the sound," explains Gore. "If the sound were within our range of hearing, just imagine a noise three times as loud as a screaming police siren randomly switching itself on and off. You certainly wouldn't bend down to have a drink or nibble something. What it does is to give the animal something similar to a migraine headache. Although the frequencies are nearly inaudible to humans, the device will even give people a headache if they stay around it too long."

This system is so new that Gore has had very few opportunities to test its effectiveness. However, those that have been completed are very promising. Peter Thompson, for example, operates a wheat farm in western Queensland that has been plagued with kangaroos. In the year before he tested Roo-Guard, Peter and his brother went kangaroo shooting on their property for 75 consecutive nights. During this period they also had commercial shooters operating in the area. At harvest time they still lost some 25 acres of wheat to the kangaroos.

Mr. Thompson's letter after the Roo-Guard test:

> The particular area I chose for the trial is one where a natural corridor of virgin scrub leads up from a creek with permanent water. I felt that if the machine would work here effectively, it would work anywhere. This is also an area where some of our best cropping soil is. . . . The 'roos and wallabies had eaten in (from the fence-line) fifteen to thirty meters [50 to 100 feet] over a nine-hundred meter strip [approximately 3,000 feet] when we put the machine in operation in June. Without having to shoot in the area throughout the season, we were thrilled to see the wheat recover with a shower of rain and grow back completely, whilst unprotected areas on the other parts of the property continued to be eaten down.

It is estimated that wheat farmers in Queensland lose over $100 million in crops to kangaroos. Widespread use of a repelling device like David Gore's would have both economic and humanitarian benefits. When commercial shooting in an area is not enough to curb the kangaroo problem, the farmers themselves will go shooting. Unfortunately, they are not as expert at shooting as the professional and often use shotguns that wound and maim. Also, some grain farmers deliberately aim for gut shots so that the wounded animal will crawl away toward cover to die. A dead kangaroo rotting in the wheat would spoil part of the crop.

To reduce kangaroo populations in an area, Mr. Gore and the CSIRO have begun experimenting with the Roo-Guard device around water holes.

"If you can keep them from water, you can keep them from grazing that general area," says Gore. "You do that, and you'll find that a gradual cull will occur instead of having to go out and shoot them. They breed to the feed, as it were."

Another successful experiment that I've recently learned of is a 'roo-proof fence for protecting watering points. First tried on a ranch in Western Australia, the fence consisted of two electrified wires, each only an inch or so off the ground, strung around a watering-trough supplied by a deep well. When the kangaroos came to drink, they would lay their tails across the two wires and receive a shock that scared them away.

Other Experimental Kangaroo Population Controls

Like most range animals, the big kangaroos will periodically come to mineral salt licks to supplement their diet. The CSIRO has been investigating this phenomenon and is reported to be developing a salt block containing a kangaroo birth control

This unfortunate kangaroo's feet became entangled in the top wires when it tried to jump the fence.

Opposite: With the proper attitudes and care, people and their technology can coexist with wildlife.

Red kangaroos being cannon-net-
ted at a stock watering trough.

agent. If it works, it may have far-reaching implications for controlling and perhaps eliminating kangaroos from entire districts.

Traditional fencing designed to keep out kangaroos is both expensive and ineffective. Kinchega National Park in western New South Wales is enclosed by a macropod "deterrent" fence 6 feet (1.8 meters) high on its south and western borders. Originally erected to prevent the dispersal of kangaroos from the park, it simply hasn't worked. Researchers studying the fence's effectiveness discovered that several of their tagged kangaroos maintained regularly visited home ranges on both sides of the boundary fence.

If you can't keep kangaroos out of an area, you can at least minimize the damage they do to fences designed for livestock. Some farmers and graziers have begun incorporating used truck tires into their fences at places where kangaroo regularly cross. This allows the animals to come and go without damaging the fence and sheep apparently will not go through the holes.

The Research Goes On

All over Australia, scientific studies are being carried out to increase our understanding of macropods and their ecology on this unique continent. A leader in this field, the University of New South Wales maintains field stations in both the dry eastern and moist western parts of the state. Because they were important locations in which to gather information, these facilities soon became my "unofficial" homes while I was in Australia. (Cowan Field Station, a 10-acre [4-hectare] compound located in the Muogamarra Nature Preserve near Sydney, and Fowlers Gap Arid

A Red kangaroo is radio-collared by a capture team at the University of New South Wales' Fowlers Gap Arid Zone Research Station.

Zone Research Station, a 97,000-acre [39,200-hectare] working sheep station north of Broken Hill, are both excellent facilities for active graduate studies.)

At Fowlers Gap, Graeme Moss, a doctoral candidate, was studying the ecology of the Red kangaroo. In order to follow an individual animal's movements, he needed to first capture it alive and unhurt and then fit it with a radio-collar and colored plastic ear tags for identification. Moss then doggedly followed the animals, day after day, in order to determine their range and to observe their social interactions.

To an outside observer, catching kangaroos was really the most exciting part of his work. There are two basic methods of capture: The first one is called "cannon-netting" and consists of a 65-by-65-foot (20-by-20-meter) square net that is attached to four projectiles. Each projectile is fitted into a cannon mounted on a fixed metal pole. The cannons are loaded with 8 grams of black powder each and a detonator that is triggered by a 12-volt car battery. The entire arrangement is set up at a watering point or some other place that kangaroos are likely to visit. A detonating wire is run out to a vehicle that is used as a blind and here you wait, sometimes for several days. When a kangaroo does show up, things happen fast. The net is fired over the animal and immediately the researchers pile out of the vehicle on the run in order to tackle and subdue the bouncing form (or forms) under the net.

"Stunning" is an even more sporting way of live capture. The technique is strictly a team effort; for the operation to be successful you need several "catchers," a "spot-lighter," a "shooter" and a driver for a four-wheel drive vehicle. The hunt begins after dark when the vehicle is driven cross-country in an area that contains a great many kangaroos. The flatter the landscape, of course, the less bumpy the ride. When a kangaroo of suitable size and sex is located, it is "held" in the spotlight while the vehicle moves towards the animal. When it is within 50 yards or so (approximately 50 meters), the driver stops. The shooter then readies his .22 caliber rifle, which is equipped with a scope and supersonic ammunition, the catchers ready on their mark for a sprint. The shooter aims and fires at a spot about an inch (3 centimeters) above the animal's skull, between its ears. Instantly, at the sound of the shot, the catchers race along both margins of the light beam towards the kangaroo and attempt to rush it from all sides.

While all of this is going on, the kangaroo stares dumbly at the spotlight, shaking its head now and then. It is thought that the sonic boom created by the projectile passing between the kangaroo's ears causes temporary deafness, so that it is unable to locate the source of further sound for about 10 to 15 seconds. Being dazzled by the spotlight also prevents it from seeing its captors clearly.

A numbered collar tag identifies this female Red kangaroo to the researcher.

Dr. Tim Clancy tracks a radio-collared kangaroo with a directional receiver.

Small kangaroos are usually caught by the tail but large animals are best subdued by a rugby- or football-style flying tackle that pins the animal to the ground. Each catcher tries to position himself to be able to intercept the kangaroo should it evade the first catcher, the spotlight following the action until capture is complete. For every successful "take" there may be five or six hilarious failures as catchers crash into each other and tumble over the ground.

Postcapture Myopathy

The subdued kangaroo is first placed in a burlap bag and then injected with Valium, 1 to 1.5 milligrams per kilogram of body weight, to calm it down and to prevent postcapture myopathy. Myopathy, or muscle degeneration, can be a serious problem when using wild kangaroos for study purposes. It is a stress-related

Above: A researcher climbs a kangaroo observation and tracking tower.

Opposite: Kangaroos will remain an important part of Australia's national folklore.

disease, characterized by the rupture of the voluntary muscle cells, and it is usually fatal. Its symptoms may not appear until two or three days after the animal has been caught, measured, weighed, collared and released in apparent good health.

"Kangaroos are surprisingly fragile," says Graeme Moss. "That's why we give them twice as much Valium as we used to and then supplement it with a shot of Vitamin E to help with inflammation. These animals are really not as tough as they look."

CONSERVING KANGAROOS: A WORLD VIEW

Today, we are realizing that even the great ecosystems—the forests, plains, deserts and oceans—of our planet are surprisingly fragile. The activities of human development and agriculture over the years have already transformed entire regions into altered environments that may not return to their pristine conditions for the rest of recorded history. Because of our power to affect nature on a global scale, the future for all wildlife, including kangaroos, is inextricably linked to that of us—the people. Even subtle changes in the way we perceive and manage our lands can have far-reaching effects for better or for worse. As our living environment steadily deteriorates from the strains of overpopulation, overdevelopment, pollution and misuse of our natural resources, the time has finally come for us, as individuals, communities, businesses, governments and as a species, to make choices that will guard against the further erosion of our planet's fragile natural heritage. We *must* learn to use the land without devastating its natural systems and its wildlife. If we do not do this, without a doubt we will continue to destroy the quality of our lives and perhaps ourselves in the end.

HAND-REARING ORPHANED KANGAROOS

This section is written especially for Australians. Each year a large number of kangaroo joeys are orphaned by weekend "sport" shooters and road accidents. Most of these youngsters are simply left behind to die, but a surprising number are picked up by caring people to be raised as pets or brought to wildlife rehabilitation centers. These mostly privately funded centers are located in every state of Australia and any local office of the National Parks and Wildlife Service can supply you with their names and addresses.

Unfortunately, most of those well-meaning people who attempt to rear an orphaned kangaroo have little or no experience in caring for native animals and consequently very few of these youngsters survive to adulthood. The following information is provided to help increase the expected survival rate of these orphans with the hope that they may be someday successfully released back into the wild.

Left: This orphaned Tammar wallaby scarcely fills a wool cap.

Opposite: Volunteer Anwan Cullen bottle-feeds a Red kangaroo joey at the Kangaroo Protection Co-Op Orphanage in Dural, New South Wales.

Before you decide to raise an orphaned joey, consider whether or not taking it to a rehab center is a viable option. (There are a lot of reasons why people decide to raise wild animals, particularly kangaroos, and I won't go into them at length. The most often-quoted reason is that the wildlife center was too far away and there was no one from the center willing or able to come out and pick up the orphan. Another major reason is simply that having a pet kangaroo sounds like a great idea.) In strict legal terms, however, you must have a permit from the Australian National Park and Wildlife Service in order to raise *any* native animal.

The two most important things you can provide a new orphan are warmth and proper food. If the joey's eyes are still closed and its skin shows pink from an almost complete lack of fur, it is too young and will be difficult to raise. At this stage, the joey's immune system is not completely developed and it is very prone to illness.

Stress also depresses the immune system, making the animal vulnerable to disease. Avoid constant handling of the joey, especially upon arrival, and do not let it become chilled by prolonged wet weather.

Occasionally a joey that is suffering from even severe hypothermia and dehydration from lack of milk can be nursed back to health. The most exceptional instance that I have seen occurred while I was making a stopover at the University of New South Wales' Cowan Field Station. Ray Williams, the manager of the facility, had been making his morning feeding rounds at the various kangaroo paddocks when he discovered a small, nearly hairless joey lying on the ground in the Red kangaroo compound. Apparently, its mother had ejected it from her pouch when she became frightened and ran into the fence. Perhaps a low-flying eagle had scared her so.

The weather had been very cool and when Ray brought the little joey into the office for examination its body was as cold as death itself. That wet, dirty little 8-inch-long infant was also covered with nasty bruises and skin abrasions suffered during its fall. It seemed hopeless to me, and Ray, who has a great deal of experience in these matters, tended to agree but he held back from destroying the animal just to put it out of its misery. He cleaned it up, wrapped it in a warm blanket and took it home with him.

"People have successfully raised pouch-young from dead mother kangaroos whose bodies are more than two days old and have begun to stink," he told me before he left.

When Ray arrived at work the next morning, I was amazed to learn that the little kangaroo had survived the night. Over the next few months I regularly received surprising reports of its progress.

Ray's wife, Anne, took over the daily care of the joey, which they named "Flicker." Flicker shared the house with two young girls and a young hand-reared Swamp wallaby.

"We almost gave up on Flicker several times," says Anne Williams, "and every time that we would threaten to 'put her down,' she would suddenly get better. She once went blind for a while and another time she developed a serious infection in her foot that we thought would be permanently crippling, but she seems okay now."

With constant care, Flicker grew into a large healthy adult and was eventually placed back in the paddock with her mother and the others. The last news that I have received of her is that she recently had become a mother herself.

Keeping the Joey Warm

Young kangaroos cannot regulate their own body temperature efficiently, so providing them with a warm artificial pouch is essential. A soft cotton pillowcase lined with a woolen baby blanket or an old sweatshirt with the arms cut off and

Amy Williams takes a young Red-necked wallaby, snuggled comfortably beneath her sweater, out for a walk.

the holes sewn closed will serve nicely. (Do not use synthetic fabrics as they seem to irritate the joey's sensitive skin.) The pillowcase with the wool liner and the joey snuggled inside should be hung with the opening facing upward on two nails or hooks on the wall of a heated porch or warm room. The bottom of the bag should just touch the floor. Artificial warmth should be provided, especially if the joey is too young to have fur. Keep the temperature just under 89° Fahrenheit (32° Centigrade) for unfurred animals and about 82° Fahrenheit (28° Centigrade) for furred ones. A hot-water bottle or electric pet blanket can be very useful for this purpose.

As a girl, Magda Cawthorn of Orange, New South Wales, raised a kangaroo in the outback of New South Wales.

"We made a pouch from a potato sack, cut a slit in it and filled it with jumpers and sweaters," she recalls. "For the first few times, we would have to physically put the joey into it, but it soon became accustomed to the procedure. It was very amusing to watch the kangaroo go in; she would first put in her head and then do a complete somersault flip inside."

When the joey is old enough to come out of its "pouch" for short periods of time, it still must be kept warm. A young Bennett's wallaby that was being raised by a family I was visiting in Tasmania would stand very close to an electrical radiant heater for several minutes before continuing its exploration of the kitchen. As soon as it felt a bit chilled, it would hop back to the heater and quickly warm up. Care should be taken to prevent direct contact with hot stoves or radiators, though, because young kangaroos appear indifferent to the effects of extreme heat and may be easily burnt.

The Right Kind of Food

When compared to cow's milk, kangaroo milk has very low lactose content. Kangaroos have trouble digesting lactose, so feedings of straight cow's milk should be avoided since it can lead to liver damage and even permanent blindness. Although there are specially formulated synthetic kangaroo milks available through certain outlets, most people will look to their local grocer store for the supplies they need to raise a joey.

Digestalac, my first choice, is a product that is commonly available in most stores and pharmacies. It is made from milk in which 95 percent of the lactose has been converted into readily absorbable glucose and galactose. Mix it as per the instructions on the tin, thicken it slightly with some baby cereal and fortify it with a drop of liquid vitamins available at any pharmacy. A baby bottle with the hole in the

Big enough to have the run of the house, a Grey kangaroo warms himself near an electric heater. The bandage on the right foot protects a stubbed toe.

nipple slightly enlarged will do well as a dispenser. I've also seen a rubber glove with a hole cut in one of the finger tips work almost as well.

If Digestalac is not available, kangaroos have been successfully raised on a diet of Carnation Evaporated Milk (not Nestle's). Mix the milk, half and half, with water and then mix in a drop or two of liquid vitamins and a half teaspoon of powdered calcium. Do not use non-milk products for the formula base. Like a human baby, a very small joey may have to be fed every two or three hours for the first week or two.

When the joey increases in size and begins poking its head out of the "pouch," its liquid diet can be augmented with bits of cooked vegetables and soft fruits. When the joey is hopping around by itself you can then offer a larger variety of fresh veggies and perhaps even some tender grass to nibble.

Continue to supplement its diet with milk until it will no longer take the bottle. (I've seen joeys that are out of the "pouch" trained to drink milk from a bowl.)

All feeding formulas should be stored in the refrigerator after mixing. Warm it to body temperature just prior to feeding. Kangaroo mothers lick their young to stimulate defecation and urination. After each feeding, gently rub the genital area with a bunched tissue. The joey will often accommodate you immediately, helping you to keep the "pouch" clean.

A symptom known as "scouring" or diarrhea is a danger signal that something is wrong with the joey's digestion. Scouring seems to occur when there is a sudden change in diet and for other less known reasons. If scouring cannot be stopped, the young kangaroo may die. Avon Browning, a woman who has successfully raised dozens of kangaroos for the National Parks Service and various zoos, has discovered that two heaping teaspoons of glucose mixed with two ounces of boiled water and fed every so often over a 24-hour period will often stop scouring. If that fails, a veterinarian can also be of help. (In Australia, veterinarians often do not charge for treating wildlife.)

As the kangaroo grows and its teeth develop, it will forego milk in favor of more substantial foods. One diet that I have known to be successful is a mixture of chicken pellets, cracked corn, sunflower seeds, wheat and a bit of charcoal. Carrots, alfalfa and dried grass should also be available. Goat pellets are good, too. Sliced apples can be given as a special treat.

A Few Other Considerations

As mentioned earlier, diarrhea is the most common ailment that can lead to the death of your kangaroo. There are, however, several other diseases that you should be aware of. Very small pouch young often get a disease known as "thrush." Some of its symptoms include: reluctance to suck; greenish, smelly, loose feces; and brownish saliva. It can be successfully treated by orally administering Mycostatin drops, which can be prescribed by a veterinarian. Dosage is about .5 milliliter for every 1.5 kilograms of 'roo. Administer three times per day for the first two days and then reduce to just .5 milliliter of medicine twice a day for up to 10 days. Improvement should be noticed within two or three days.

Several types of bacterial infections can usually be traced to poor hygiene. The most common are pneumonia and coccidiosis. For some reason coccidiosis is a frequent cause of death in captive Grey kangaroos. One other disease to look out for is called "lumpy-jaw." This disease can occur to kangaroos that are fed coarse-stemmed hay. According to J. D. Wallach's report in the *International Zoo and Yearbook*, ". . . the disease appears to be associated with trauma to the oral mucosa by the mechanical abrasion of the rough forage. This allows the causative organism *Nocardia spp.* entry into the soft tissue of the mandible or maxilla. The

organism may be found as a normal resident of the kangaroo's mouth or in the soil of the enclosure."

Lumpy-jaw is characterized by a swelling of the jaw and can lead to death if the jaw bone is invaded. Both coccidiosis and lumpy-jaw are diseases that are only marginally treatable and therefore should be left to a veterinarian's care.

When transporting kangaroos, either for release or other purposes, use a crate or large box with good ventilation. Overheating during transport can be fatal. Be sure the cage is large enough to allow the animal to lie on some bedding and if it is going to be a long trip, food and water should be provided. You can also use Valium to tranquilize the animal during transport.

One final word: Kangaroos can be remarkably engaging pets, but males of the larger species often become dangerously aggressive when they are about five years old, especially around children. These animals should be released or given to a rehabilitation center before they become unmanageable.

KANGAROO SPECIES AND THEIR CONSERVATION STATUS

1. Musky rat-kangaroo (*Hypsiprymnodon moschatus*): Vulnerable. Limited range in rainforest areas in and around Atherton tablelands, Queensland.
2. Long-nosed potoroo (*Potorous tridactylus*): Common. Occurs in moist habitats of eastern Australia, including Tasmania.
3. Broad-faced potoroo (*Potorous platyops*): Last seen in 1875, now considered extinct.
4. Long-footed potoroo (*Potorous longipes*): Endangered. Recently discovered (described in 1981), it has a limited range in southeastern Victoria.

Rufous bettong.

5. Burrowing bettong (*Bettongia lesueur*): Rare. Exists only on a few islands off the coast of northwestern Australia.
6. Brush-tailed bettong (*Bettongia penicillata*): Endangered. Found only in a few tiny areas in southwestern Western Australia.
7. Queensland bettong (*Bettongia tropica*): Vulnerable. Range may be limited to small area of northeastern Queensland.
8. Tasmanian bettong (*Bettongia gaimardi*): Common but vulnerable. Found throughout eastern half of Tasmania. Extinct on mainland of Australia.
9. Desert rat-kangaroo (*Caloprymnus campestris*): Possibly extinct. Last seen in 1935.
10. Rufous bettong (*Aepyprymnus rufescens*): Common. Range includes eastern Queensland.
11. Banded hare-wallaby (*Lagostrophus fasciatus*): Endangered. Apparently extinct on mainland, now only found on three offshore islands of Western Australia.
12. Rufous hare-wallaby (*Lagorchestes hirsutus*): Endangered. Small populations found in Tanami Desert of central Australia and on two offshore islands of Western Australia.
13. Eastern hare-wallaby (*Lagorchestes leporides*): Extinct. Last recorded sighting was in 1890.
14. Spectacled hare-wallaby (*Lagorchestes conspicillatus*): Secure. Widespread in northern Queensland (except on the York Peninsula) and in the Northern Territory.
15. Central hare-wallaby (*Lagorchestes asomatus*): Possibly extinct. Known only by one skull collected in 1932 in central Australia.
16. Crescent nail-tail wallaby (*Onychogalea lunata*): Presumed extinct. One was recorded to have been seen in the Northern Territory in 1956.
17. Bridled nail-tail wallaby (*Onychogalea fraenata*): Endangered. Found only in a small area of eastern Queensland.

Red-legged pademelon.

18. Northern nail-tail wallaby (*Onychogalea unguifera*): Secure. Occupies most of northern Australia.

19. Tasmanian pademelon (*Thylogale billardierii*): Common. Found primarily in Tasmania. No longer occurs on mainland Australia.

20. Red-necked pademelon (*Thylogale thetis*): Common. Occurs in rainforest areas of southeastern Queensland and northeastern New South Wales.

21. Red-legged pademelon (*Thylogale stigmatica*): Secure but not common. Found throughout coastal eastern Australia, north to the York Peninsula and southern New Guinea.

Red-necked pademelon.

Bridled nail-tailed wallaby.

22. Dusky pademelon (*Thylogale brunii*): Common. Occurs throughout the eastern two-thirds of New Guinea.
23. Black dorcopsis (*Dorcopsis atrata*): Vulnerable, possibly endangered. Has a restricted range on a small island near New Guinea.
24. Brown dorcopsis (*Dorcopsis veterum*): Secure. Inhabits lowland rainforest in southern half of New Guinea.
25. Grey dorcopsis (*Dorcopsis luctuosa*): Common. Inhabits coastal forests of eastern New Guinea.
26. White-striped dorcopsis (*Dorcopsis hageni*): Common. Occurs in lowland rainforests of northern New Guinea.

27. Little dorcopsis (*Dorcopsulus vanheurni*): Common. Inhabits montane forests along length of the New Guinean Cordilla Range.
28. Macleay's dorcopsis (*Dorcopsulus macleayi*): Rare. Found in eastern New Guinea.
29. Quokka (*Setonix brachyurus*): Vulnerable. Rare on mainland (southwestern Western Australia) but common on Rottnest and Bald Islands offshore.
30. Nabarlek (*Peradorcas concinna*): Rare. Occurs in northern Western Australia and Northern Territory.
31. Monjon (*Petrogale burbidgei*): Vulnerable. Discovered in the 1970s, its known range is limited to a small area of northern Western Australia.
32. Rothschild's rock-wallaby (*Petrogale rothschildi*): Secure. Found in the Hamersley Range of Western Australia and on two offshore islands.
33. Unadorned rock-wallaby (*Petrogale inornata*): Secure but uncommon. Occurs in northeastern Queensland and on Great Palm and Magnetic islands.
34. Proserpine rock-wallaby (*Petrogale persephone*): Endangered. Discovered in 1976, it is found only in the Proserpine district of eastern Queensland.

Yellow-footed rock-wallaby.

35. Godman's rock-wallaby (*Petrogale godmani*): Vulnerable. Occurs in the eastern half of the York Peninsula near Cooktown in Queensland.
36. Short-eared rock-wallaby (*Petrogale brachyotis*): Common. Found in northern Western Australia and Northern Territory.
37. Brush-tailed rock-wallaby (*Petrogale penicillata*): Common. Found in eastern and southeastern Australia.
38. Black-footed rock-wallaby (*Petrogale lateralis*): Vulnerable and usually rare. Occurs in central Australia in the Kimberley and MacDonnell Ranges.
39. Yellow-footed rock-wallaby (*Petrogale xanthropus*): Vulnerable but common in isolated areas. Found in Flinders Ranges of South Australia, western New South Wales and southwestern Queensland.
40. Allied rock-wallaby (*Petrogale assimilis*): Limited range. Isolated colonies found on rocky outcrops and gorges in northeastern Queensland.

Agile wallaby.

Antilopine wallaroo.

41. Swamp wallaby (*Wallabia bicolor*): Common. Found throughout eastern and southeastern Australia.
42. Parma wallaby (*Macropus parma*): Rare and possibly vulnerable. Patchy range in eastern New South Wales.
43. Tammar wallaby (*Macropus eugenii*): Vulnerable. Occurs in a small area in southwestern South Australia, scattered populations in Western Australia and on several offshore islands, including Kangaroo Island.
44. Toolache wallaby (*Macropus greyi*): Presumed extinct. No specimens have been obtained since 1924.
45. Black-gloved wallaby (*Macropus irma*): Common. Occurs in open forests of southwestern Western Australia.
46. Whiptail wallaby (*Macropus parryi*): Common. Found in eastern Queensland and northeastern New South Wales.
47. Black-striped wallaby (*Macropus dorsalis*): Common in localized areas. Occurs in southeastern Queensland and northeastern New South Wales.
48. Red-necked wallaby (*Macropus rufogriseus*): Common. Found from southeastern Queensland, south through the coastal forests to southern Victoria and Tasmania.
49. Agile wallaby (*Macropus agilis*): Common. Ranges throughout Northern Australia (especially in coastal areas) and in southern New Guinea.
50. Western grey kangaroo (*Macropus fuliginosus*): Common. Found over southern one-third of Australia except for coastal ranges of New South Wales and Victoria.

51. Eastern grey kangaroo (*Macropus giganteus*): Common. Found throughout eastern one fourth of Australia, from northern Queensland to Tasmania.
52. Common wallaroo or Euro (*Macropus robustus*): Common. Wide-ranging over Australia but restricted to hilly or mountainous country.
53. Black wallaroo (*Macropus bernardus*): Vulnerable and rare. Occurs almost exclusively in the Arnhem Land area of Northern Territory.
54. Antilopine wallaroo (*Macropus antilopinus*): Common. Occurs throughout "top-end" (northern) Australia.
55. Red kangaroo (*Macropus rufus*): Common. Occurs over nearly two-thirds of arid Australia.
56. Bennett's tree-kangaroo (*Dendrolagus bennettianus*): Vulnerable. Range has contracted to the Daintree River area of northeastern Queensland.
57. Lumholtz's tree-kangaroo (*Dendrolagus lumholtzi*): Vulnerable. Occurs in isolated patches of remnant rainforest in northeastern Queensland.
58. Grizzled tree-kangaroo (*Dendrolagus inustus*): Rare and probably vulnerable. Found in hill forests in extreme western and northwestern New Guinea.
59. Goodfellow's tree-kangaroo (*Dendrolagus goodfellowi*): Uncommon. Occurs in oak and beech forests of eastern New Guinea.
60. Matchie's tree-kangaroo (*Dendrolagus matchiei*): Vulnerable. Found only on the Huon Peninsula of northern New Guinea.
61. Doria's tree-kangaroo (*Dendrolagus dorianus*): Uncommon. Occurs in the upland rainforests of New Guinea.
62. Vogelkop tree-kangaroo (*Dendrolagus ursinus*): Uncommon. Restricted to the Vogelkop Peninsula of western New Guinea.
63. Scott's tree-kangaroo (*Dendrolagus scottae*): Endangered. Restricted to mossy forest above 3,900 feet (1,200 meters) on the North Coast Range, Papua New Guinea. Its total known habitat area is estimated to be only about 10 to 15 square miles (25 to 40 square kilometers).

A trio of Grey kangaroos hop into a grove eucalyptus trees.

FURTHER READING

A fter having read practically everything about kangaroos published during the past 15 to 20 years, I have come to the conclusion that, outside of a few children's books, there is very little material on this subject readily available for the general reader. The following works are among the few that I can recommend. Unfortunately, many of them are out of print and can only be found in large libraries:

Archer, Michael, and Georgina Clayton, eds. *Vertebrate Zoogeography and Evolution in Australia*. Sydney: Hesperian Press, 1985. A collection of biological essays tracing the evolution of wildlife in Australia. Contains some humorous illustrations.

Archer, Michael, with Tim Flannery and Gordon Grigg. *The Kangaroo*. Sydney: Weldons Pty. Ltd, 1985. A general book about macropods and their evolution with species-by-species accounts.

Australian Zoologist. Journal of the Royal Zoological Society of New South Wales, Vol. 24, No. 3, August 1988. Entire issue is dedicated to kangaroo harvesting and the conservation of arid and semi-arid lands.

Frith, H. J., and J. H. Calaby. *Kangaroos*. Melbourne: F. W. Cheshire Publishing, 1969. A dated but classic book about the Red kangaroo.

Grigg, Gordon, Peter Jarman, and Ian Hume, eds. *Kangaroos, Wallabies and Rat-kangaroos*. Sydney: Surrey Beatty and Sons, 1989. Vol. 1 and 2. A collection of scientific papers of recent work concerning macropods.

Haigh, Christine, ed. *Kangaroos and Other Macropods of New South Wales*. Sydney: New South Wales National Parks and Wildlife Service, 1981. Written by various scientists, this is an informative but dated collection of essays and photographs.

Hand, Susanne J., ed. *Care and Handling of Australian Native Animals*. Sydney: Surrey Beatty and Sons, 1990. Contains an excellent section, written by Ray Williams, on keeping kangaroos in captivity.

Kangaroo Management Programs of the Australian States. Canberra: Australian National Parks and Wildlife Service, 1984. Details management and culling programs on a state-by-state basis. Good overall view but slightly dated.

Poignant, Axel. *The Improbable Kangaroo*. Sydney: Angus and Robertson, 1965. Contains a good narrative on the history of the discovery of the kangaroo.

Strahan, Ronald, ed. *Complete Book of Australian Mammals*. Sydney: Angus and Robertson, 1983. An exhaustive encyclopedia of Australian mammals with a good section on macropods.

Vandenbeld, John. *Nature of Australia: A Portrait of the Island Continent*. New York: Facts On File, 1988. A good general account of Australian natural history, including kangaroos.

INDEX

Black-gloved wallaby (*Macropus irma*) 187

Black-striped wallaby (*Macropus dorsalis*) 93, 187

Black wallaroo (*Macropus bernardus*) 117, 123, 125, 188

blood 76, 95

blood supply
　　to forelimbs 44
　　to pouch 29

"blue-fliers" 125

body temperature 22, 44–45, 127, 176

bonding *38*, 56–57, 70, 109, 125

Bonthrone, Bill 53, 149

Boodie Island 75

boomerangs 134

Borderwatch (newspaper) 137

botfly larvae 53

bounding 8

bounty payments 102, 143

boxing 59

Bracken fern 87

breeding cycle 30–31
　　grey kangaroos 120
　　hare-wallabies 81
　　pademelons 83
　　Quokka 79
　　rat-kangaroos 70
　　rock-wallabies 99–100
　　Swamp wallaby 87
　　tree-kangaroos 109

Bridled nail-tail wallaby (*Onychogalea fraenata*) 80, 81, 182, *184*

Britain *see* Great Britain

Broad-faced potoroo (*Potorous platyops*) 71, 181

Brown dorcopsis (*Dorcopsis veterum*) 86, 184

Browning, Avon 179

browsing 8, 23, 48, 79, 81, 86–87

Brush-tailed bettong (*Bettongia penicillata*) 36, 73–74, *74*, 182

Brush-tailed rock-wallaby (*Petrogale penicillata*) 15, *98*, 99, *103*, 186

Bryant, Chris 155

Burrowing bettong (*Bettongia lesueur*) 16, 75, 159, 182

bushfires *see* wildfires

"bush tucker" 135

C

caecum 20

Caloprymnus campestris see Desert rat-kangaroo

camels 14

"cannon-netting" *168*, 170

Cape York Peninsula 83, 87

capillary network 22, 127

captive breeding programs 72, 80, 88, 115

capture, live *168*, 170–171

carbohydrates 20, 37

cardiovascular system 14, 18, 44, 127, 130, 161 *see also* capillary network

"catchers" 170–171

cats (feral) 65, 70, 73, 80, 159, 161

cattle
　　digestive system similarity 8, 20
　　habitat destruction by 79, 81, 90, 151
　　killing zones and 148
　　stock routes as kangaroo habitat 159

cave paintings 134–135

caves 44, *44*, 47, 99–100, 102, *122*, 122–123, 130, 134

Cawthorn, Magda 177

cellulose 20, 70, 76, 99

Central Cordillera 85

Central hare-wallaby (*Lagorchestes asomatus*) 79, 182

chemical signals 109, 125

chickens 114, 147

cholesterol 147

chromosomes 87, 95

Clancy, Tim 53, 56, 93, 127, *171*

classification **12**, 67, 87, 95, 134

claws
　　babies born with 35
　　feeding function 11, 48
　　fighting function 57, 59
　　grooming function 23, 68
　　tree-climbing function 107

climate change 7–8, 11–12 *see also* drought

climbing 107

cloaca 28, 30, 76

clubs (hunting) 135

coccidiosis 52, 179–180

cockatoos 49, 133

cockroaches 86

Collie, Alexander 28, 36, 89

coloration and markings
　　dorcopsis wallabies 86
　　grey kangaroos 118–119
　　hare-wallabies 80
　　Macropus wallabies 92–93
　　nail-tail wallabies 81
　　Red kangaroo 125, *126*
　　rock-wallabies 99–101, *101*
　　tree-kangaroos 110, 114
　　wallaroos 122

color perception 51

commercial uses 141–153, 156

Common Wallaroo (Euro) (*Macropus robustus*) 6, *121–122*, 122–123
　　adaptation to aridity 18, 44, 49, 130
　　classification 117
　　conservation status 188
　　home area 47, 130
　　hunting quotas 148
　　infancy 36, 123
　　range 188
　　reproduction 31, 123
　　vocal repertoire 61

Commonwealth Scientific and Industrial Research Organisation (CSIRO) 139, 162, 167

communication *see* signals; sounds

competition
　　for caves 102, 122

from goats 102
　　between males 120
　　from rabbits 16, 138
　　from sheep 16

Compound 1080 (sodium monofluoroacetate) 119, 160–161

conservation groups 96, 140–141, 148

conservation status of species 181–188

continental drift 4–5

continuous breeding 83

Cook, Captain James 3

cooling mechanisms *see* temperature regulation

copulation *see* mating

coursing clubs (hunting) 137

courtship 30–31, 52, 70, 76, 120–121

Cowan Field Station 169, 176

"crawl walk" 23, *24*, 68

crepuscular activity 47

Crescent nail-tail wallaby (*Onychogalea lunata*) 81, 182

Cretaceous Period 7

crocodiles 8, 92, 135

crows 62

CSIRO *see* Commonwealth Scientific and Industrial Research Organisation

Cullen, Anwan *174*

culling 140, 148–149, 153, 155–156, 160, 167

Cutta Cutta Cave 100

D

Daintree Rainforest *104*, 105–106

Dampier Archipelago 101

Dawson, Terry 14, 20, 23, 44–45, 127

day camps 93

de Bruijn, C. 83

deer 51, 117, 119, 141

defecation 36, 179

dehydration 14, 44, 127, 130, 176

Dendrolagus bennettianus see Bennett's tree-kangaroo

Dendrolagus dorianus see Doria's tree-kangaroo

Dendrolagus goodfellowi see Goodfellow's tree-kangaroo

Dendrolagus inustus see Grizzled tree-kangaroo

Dendrolagus lumholtzi see Lumholtz's tree-kangaroo

Dendrolagus matchiei see Matchie's tree-kangaroo

Dendrolagus scottae see Scott's tree-kangaroo

Dendrolagus ursinus see Vogelkop tree-kangaroo

dentition *see* teeth

desert
　　foxes as predators in 162
　　home to
　　　　hare-wallabies 79
　　　　nail-tail wallabies 81
　　　　Red kangaroo 14, 117, 125, 127
　　land degradation 151

molars 19, 76, 100
monitors (lizards) 65
Monjon (*Petrogale burbidgei*) 100, 185
monkeys 106–107
mortality rate 48, 160
mosaic land burning 134
Moss, Graeme 31, 126, 170
mother-daughter bonds 57
motifs 134
mulga forests 60
Muogamarra Nature Preserve 169
muscle control 29
muscle degeneration 171–172
mushrooms 19
musk glands 69
muskrats 141
Musky rat-kangaroo (*Hypsiprymnodon moschatus*) 68, 68–70
 classification 12
 conservation status 181
 diurnal activity 47, 70
 early species resemblance 8, 68
 pregnancy pattern 32
 range 181
 twin births 28, 70
mycorrhizal fungi 74
myopathy 171–172
myxomatosis 147

N

Nabarlek (*Peradorcas concinna*) 20, 100, 185
nail-tail wallabies 80, 81–82, 182–183, 184
National Farmer's Federation (Australia) 148–149
national parks 48, 96, 103, 157–159
National Parks and Wildlife Service (Australia) 79, 81, 140, 148, 157, 175–176, 179
Natural History (journal) 107
natural selection 14
Nature of Australia, The (John Vandenbeld) 8
nematode worms 21, 52–53, 53
nervous system 161
nests 67, 69–70, 73, 75
nets 81, 134
New Guinea *see also* Papua New Guinea
 geographical link to Australia 9
 habitat loss 115
 home to
  dorcopsis wallabies 14, 83, 86
  Macropus wallabies 91
  pademelons 83
  tree-kangaroos 12, 107, 110, 112, 114
 physical features 85
Newsome, Alan 126
New South Wales
 agricultural damage 139–140
 deterrent fences 169
 home to
  grey kangaroos 118

Macropus wallabies 15, 56, 88, 90, 93
 pademelons 83
 rat-kangaroos 72
 rock-wallabies 103
 tree-kangaroos 107
 industrial uses in 143, 147, 155
 rainforest logging 159
 road-kills 163
New South Wales, University of 31, 122, 169, 176
New South Wales Society 2
New Zealand 12, 15, 87–88, 93
nitrogen 20, 70, 119, 130
nocturnal activity 47, 53, 70, 73, 100, 117
nocturnal vision 51, 52
noises *see* sounds
Northern nail-tail wallaby (*Onychogalea unguifera*) 82, 183
Northern Territory (Australia) 135, 147, 159
Norway 148
nose 35, 53, 72, 86, 119 *see also* smell, sense of
Nullarbor Caves 71

O

Oahu (Hawaii) 99
observation and tracking towers 172
O'Dea, Kerin 147
odor
 of grey kangaroos 119
 of Long-footed potoroo 72
 of Musky rat-kangaroo 69
oestrus 30–32, 57
 dorcopsis wallabies 86
 grey kangaroos 118, 120–121
 Red kangaroo 130
 tree-kangaroos 110
 wallaroos 123, 125
Olson, Molly 149
omnivores 20, 67
Onion grass 82
Onychogalea fraenata see Bridled nail-tail wallaby
Onychogalea lunata see Crescent nail-tail wallaby
Onychogalea unguifera see Northern nail-tail wallaby
opossums 7, 12, 49–50
overcrowding 48, 160

P

"paddymalla" (Aboriginal term) 82
pademelons 14, 39, 82, 82–83, 84, 85, 106, 159–160, 182, 183, 183–184
pair bonds 56–57, 70
Pangaea (early continent) 4–5
panting 22, 44
Paperbark tree 136
Papua New Guinea 86, 110, 112, 115, 148
parasites 21, 52–53, 62, 160

parks, national *see* national parks
Parma wallaby (*Macropus parma*) 17, 31, 34, 88, 88, 162, 187
Pelsaert, Francisco 3, 28, 88
Penant, T. 3–4
penis 30–31
pentapedal walk 23, 24, 68
Peradorcas concinna see Nabarlek
pesticides 119
pet food 140, 147
Petrogale assimilis see Allied rock-wallaby
Petrogale brachyotis see Short-eared rock-wallaby
Petrogale burbidgei see Monjon
Petrogale godmani see Godman's rock-wallaby
Petrogale inornata see Unadorned rock-wallaby
Petrogale lateralis see Black-footed rock-wallaby
Petrogale penicillata see Brush-tailed rock-wallaby
Petrogale persephone see Proserpine rock-wallaby
Petrogale rothschildi see Rothschild's rock-wallaby
Petrogale xanthropus see Yellow-footed rock-wallaby
pheromones 125
physical differences (male/female) *see* sex differences
pigeons 49
pigs 159–161
pit traps 12, 134
placenta 6–7
plague species 76
plains *see* grassland
platypuses 6
Pleistocene Epoch 11
pneumonia 179
poisoning 74–75, 93, 119, 160–161
Poole, Bill 3, 16, 119
population *see also* culling
 influences
  Dingo removal 63
  drought 18, 32–33
  poisoning 160
  sandfly plague 53
 statistics
  hare-wallabies 80
  nail-tail wallabies 81
  rat-kangaroos 68, 70, 73–74, 76
  Red kangaroo 18, 125, 127
  rock-wallabies 15, 103
  tree-kangaroos 114–115
  wallaroos 123
 surveys
  aerial and ground 143, 148
  road-kill 163
population crashes 131
porpoises 50
Potoroidae (potoroids) *see* rat-kangaroos
potoroos 19, 69, 70–72, 71, 181